T0125262

priests & politicians

priests & politicians

The Mafia of the Soul

"For five thousand years the politician and
the priest have been in the same business."

Copyright © 1987, 2016 OSHO International Foundation
www.osho.com/copyrights

Osho image Copyright © OSHO International Foundation

All rights reserved. No part of this book may be reproduced or transmitted in any form or
by any means, electronic or mechanical, including photocopying, recording, or by any
information storage and retrieval system, without prior written permission from the
publisher.

This is a new and expanded edition created from various talks by Osho, given to a live
audience. All of Osho's talks have been published in full as books, and are also available as
original audio recordings. Audio recordings and the complete text archive can be found via
the online OSHO Library at www.osho.com/library

OSHO and SPIRITUALLY INCORRECT are registered trademarks of Osho International
Foundation www.osho.com/trademarks

OSHO MEDIA INTERNATIONAL
New York • Zurich • Mumbai
an imprint of
OSHO INTERNATIONAL
www.osho.com/oshointernational

Distributed by Publishers Group Worldwide
www.pgw.com

Library of Congress Catalog-In-Publication Data is available

Printed in India by Manipal Technologies Limited, Karnataka

ISBN: 978-1-938755-88-0
This title is also available in eBook format ISBN: 978-0-88050-070-8

CONTENTS

PROLOGUE

Now, for the first time, the world is coming close to a global death…

Up to now it was only an individual death; the society continued, the world continued. Yes, people came and went away – old people disappearing, young children coming up – but the continuity was there, life was always there. Yes, individual life has been a problem, but only the individual was concerned about it.

The priest was capable of exploiting the individual very easily. He is so weak and so small, so limited, and he knows that he is going to die – he has to seek the priest's help to find something to cling to which is undying, eternal, which will take him beyond death, and the priest has been promising that. But it was never a problem that the whole society was confronted with.

Today, now, the whole of humanity is confronted with the problem. Such a crisis has never happened before; hence pseudo-religions, pygmy religions, were enough. Small doses were needed for individuals. For the first time we are close to the death of the whole of humanity – not only the whole of humanity but the whole of life as such.

Death encountering life in its totality makes the time right for a new spirituality or new religiousness to be born.

CHAPTER 1

Religion – Real and Pseudo

The word *religion* is beautiful. It comes from a root which means bringing together those who have fallen apart in their ignorance; bringing them together, waking them up so that they can see they are not separate. Then you cannot hurt even a tree. Then your compassion and your love will be just spontaneous – not cultivated, not something of a discipline. If love is a discipline, it is false. If nonviolence is cultivated, it is false. If compassion is nurtured, it is false. But if they come spontaneously, without any effort of your own, then they have a reality so deep, so exquisite….

In the name of religion so much crime has been done in the past. More people have been killed by religious people than by anybody else. Certainly all these religions have been fake, pseudo.

The authentic religion has yet to be born.

What is religion? What is your opinion of organized religion?

Religion is the highest flight of human consciousness – it is the individual search for truth. The inner truth cannot be made an object of common knowledge. Each person has to go within himself; each time it is a new discovery. It does not matter how many people have attained awakening, realization; the moment *you* attain it, it will be absolutely fresh – because it cannot be borrowed.

The search basically consists of knowing your interiority. You have an outside, and no outside can exist without an inside: the very existence of the outside is proof of an inner world.

The inner world consists of three layers: thoughts are the most superficial; feelings are deeper – and then is the being, which is your godliness. To know one's own godliness, to know one's own eternity, is the basic search of religion.

All your senses lead you outside: the eyes open to look outside, the ears hear what is happening outside, your hands can touch what is outside. The senses are the doors to go out – and always remember, the door that takes you out can also take you in. It is the same door from which you go out of your home and through which you come back in; just the direction changes.

To go out, you need open eyes. To come in, you need closed eyes, all your senses silent. The first encounter is with the mind – but that is not your reality. Although it is inside your skull, it is not you – it is the reflection of the outside. All your thoughts are reflections of the outside. For example, a blind man cannot think about colors because he has not seen colors – hence the reflection is not possible. The blind man cannot even see darkness. Because he has never seen light or darkness outside, there is no possibility of any reflection. The blind man does not know whether there is darkness or there is light – both words are meaningless.

If you analyze your thoughts, you will find they are all triggered inside you by outside reality – so they are basically of the outside, reflected in your inner lake of consciousness. But because of these thoughts… They are a tremendous crowd in you; they go on accumulating, they create Wall of China. You have to go beyond your thoughts. Religion knows only one method – there are different names, but the method is one: it is watchfulness, it is witnessing. You simply watch your thoughts with no judgment – no condemnation, no appreciation, utterly aloof – you just see the process of thoughts passing on the screen of your mind. As your watcher becomes stronger, thoughts become less – in the same proportion. If the watcher is ten percent of your energy, then ninety percent of your energy is wasted in thoughts; if your watcher becomes ninety percent, then only ten percent remains in thoughts. The moment you are one hundred percent a watcher, the mind becomes empty.

This whole process is known as meditation. As you pass through the thoughts, you will come to the second layer which is inside you – of feelings, of your heart, which is more subtle. But by now, your watcher is capable even of watching your moods, your sentiments, your emotions, your feelings – howsoever subtle they may be. This same method works in the same way as it worked with the thoughts: soon there will be no sentiments, no feelings, no moods. You have gone beyond the mind, and the heart. Now there is utter silence; nothing moves. This is your being; this is you.

The taste of your being is truth. The beauty of your being is the beauty of existence. The silence of your being is the language that existence understands. And just to be settled in being, you have come home. The wandering is finished. The struggle is finished. At ease, you sit silently within yourself. A great hidden splendor is revealed to you: you are not separate from reality, you are one with it. The trees and the moon and the stars and the mountains are all part of one organic unity; you are also part of that organic unity – you become part of God.

Religion is man's highest achievement. Beyond religion, there is nothing – but there is no need, either. Your being is so abundant, so overflowing with bliss, silence, peace, understanding, ecstasy, that for the first time life becomes really a song, a dance, a celebration. Those who do not know religion don't know celebration.

But organized religion is a totally different affair. I have to make it clear to you that authentic religion is always individual. The moment truth is organized, it dies; it becomes a doctrine, a theology, a philosophy – but it is no longer an experience, because the crowd cannot experience. Experience happens only to individuals – separately.

It is almost like love. You cannot have organizations of love, so that you need not bother: the organization will take care, the priest will love on your behalf. But that's what has happened to religion. Each time a man discovers the truth, immediately one of the most cunning parts of humanity, the priests, surround him. They start compiling his words; they start interpreting his words; and they start making it clear to people that if you want to know truth, you have to go via them – they are agents of God. They may call themselves prophets, they may call themselves messengers; they may choose any name, but the reality is that they are self-appointed agents of God. They don't know God, but in the name of God they exploit humanity.

Organized religion is another form of politics. Just as I have always condemned politics as the lowest activity of human beings, the same is my attitude about organized religions. You can see it: the priests and the politicians have always been in conspiracy against humanity. They

> *"You can see it: the priests and the politicians have always been in conspiracy against humanity."*

have been supporting each other. They have divided life between themselves so that your worldly life belongs to the politician, he is the ruler here, and your inner life belongs to the priest, he is the ruler there.

One sometimes feels so amazed! It seems unbelievable that even in the twentieth century the pope could declare that to communicate with God directly is a sin. You should go through the priest, the right channel – because if people start going directly to God, confessing to God, praying to God, the millions of priests will be unemployed. They don't do anything; their whole function is to deceive you. Because you don't understand the language of God, and you are not so evolved, just for some fee – a donation to their church or to their temple – they will do the job for you.

All those donations go into the pockets of the priests! They don't know anything about God, but they are very learned – they can repeat scriptures like parrots. But their inner desire is not for God, not for truth – they are not seekers, they are exploiters.

I have heard…

A priest bought two parrots and he taught them, with great hardship, beautiful statements of Jesus Christ. Everybody was really amazed – the parrots were so accurate. He also made small beads for them so they were constantly praying, and he also found small Bibles for them; they always kept their Bibles open, and were counting their beads. Although they could not read, they had already crammed everything. The priest would open the page and say, "Twelfth page," and they would start reading it – not that they were reading; they had memorized it.

The priest was very pleased and he felt it would be good to have one more parrot. Rather than learning the Bible and the beads, he could be taught to give whole sermons. He found a parrot, and the pet shop owner said, "Your wish will be fulfilled; this parrot is the most intelligent I have ever seen."

But he was not aware that it was a female parrot. As the parrot was put in the same cage as the other two parrots that were counting their beads and reading the Bible, they both looked at the female parrot, and one parrot said to the other, "George, now drop those beads! Our prayers have been heard."

Your priests are no more than parrots, and their prayers are for power, for prestige, for money. They are politicians in disguise; they are doing politics in the name of God – the politics of numbers. There are now over a billion Catholics; naturally the pope is the most powerful religious man in the world.

Every religion has been trying to increase its population by different methods. Mohammedans are allowed to marry four women so that they can produce four children per year. And they have been successful: they are the second-largest religion after Christianity.

Organized religion is only a contentless, meaningless name; hidden inside is the politics of numbers. You know perfectly well – as the election comes near in India, your politicians start going to see the *shankaracharya*. For five years, nobody goes to visit the *shankaracharya*, but when the election comes near then the prime minister goes to visit the *shankaracharya*. He goes for a pilgrimage to the temples, high and deep in the mountains of the Himalayan range. For what? Suddenly, a great religious urge has arisen – which subsides as the election ends.

These people need votes; they have to pay respect to the leaders of religions. And a *shankaracharya* feels great that the prime minister is touching his feet. The followers of the *shankaracharya*, the Hindus, feel that "our prime minister is a very religious person." When the pope comes to India, even the president and the prime minister with his whole cabinet stand in line at the airport to receive him. For what? The third-largest religion in India is now Christianity, and to pay respect to the pope means all the votes of the Christians will be yours.

Organized religions – whether it is Christianity or Hinduism or Mohammedanism – have not been seekers of truth. In two thousand years, what truth has organized Christianity added to the statements of Jesus? So what is the need of this organization? It is not increasing religiousness in the world, it is simply repeating what Jesus has said – which is available in books for anybody to read. In twenty-five centuries, how many Buddhists have searched for the truth, or have found the truth? Just a long line of parrots repeating what Gautam Buddha has found.

> *"Truth has always been found by individuals. That is the privilege of the individual, and his dignity."*

You should remember that Gautam Buddha was not part of any organized religion; neither was Mahavira part of any organized religion, nor was Jesus part of any organized religion – they were individual seekers. Truth has always been found by individuals. That is the privilege of the individual, and his dignity.

Organized religions have created wars – just as politicians have done. Their names may be different: politicians fight for Socialism, for Communism, for Fascism, for Nazism, and organized religions have been fighting for God, for love, for their concept of what truth is. Millions of people have been killed in the clashes between Christians and Mohammedans, between Christians and Jews, between Mohammedans and Hindus, between Hindus and Buddhists.

Religion has nothing to do with war; it is a search for peace. But organized religions are not interested in peace – they are interested in becoming more and more powerful and dominant.

I condemn the organized religions in the same way I condemn the politicians because they are nothing but politics. When I have said to you that religious people should be respected, honored – the politicians should go to them for advice – I was not talking about organized religions; I was talking only about religious individuals. A religious individual is neither Hindu nor Christian nor Mohammedan. How can he be? God himself is not Hindu, not Mohammedan, not Christian. And the man who knows something of the divine becomes colored with his divinity, becomes fragrant with godliness. In the ancient East these religious people were our highest flowers, and even kings and emperors used to go to them to touch their feet and to be blessed – to ask their advice on problems which they were unable to solve.

If we want the world to remain alive, we have to bring back our ancient childhood days when the religious person had no interest of his own. That's why his eyes were clear, his heart was pure love; his being was nothing but a blessing. Whomsoever came to him was healed, his problems were solved; he was imparted new insights into rotten old problems.

Organized religions should disappear from the world – they should drop this mask of being religious. They are simply politicians, wolves hiding themselves in the skin of sheep. They should come into their true colors; they should be politicians – there is no harm in that. And all the time they *are* politicians, but they are playing the game in the name of religion.

Organized religions don't have any future. They should drop their disguise and come truly out in front as politicians, and be part of the political world so that we can find the authentic religious individual – who will be very rare. But just a few authentic religious individuals can lead the whole world toward light, toward immortal life, toward ultimate truth.

❖

What is the role of renunciation in your vision of religion?

The idea of renunciation is one of the fundamentals of all pseudo-religions. Its phenomenology has to be understood very deeply.

All the religions have been preaching a division between this world and the world that is beyond death, between the body and the soul. The body belongs to this world, the soul belongs to that world; hence if you want to achieve the world beyond death, which is eternal, and the happiness there is unending, then the happiness here is not worth calling happiness: it is momentary, it is dream stuff. It comes, and even before you have been able to grasp it, it is gone. It is illusory; it is a kind of mirage in the desert.

When you are far away you see a lake of water. You are thirsty and great hope arises in you. And the lake is absolutely real as far as you can see, because the proof of its reality, that water is there, is that the trees are being reflected in the water. If there is a mountain by the side, the mountain is reflected in the lake, the sun is reflected in the lake. What more proof do you need? Without water these reflections cannot happen. You rush with great hope, but as you come nearer, you find the lake is receding; the distance between you and the lake remains the same.

It was just an illusion created by sunrays reflected back from the hot desert sand. When sunrays are reflected back, they move like waves, and their movement from far away creates the illusion of water. And in their wave-like movement they attain the quality of reflecting things; they become just like a mirror. That is one half of the mirage.

The other half is in your thirst. If you were not thirsty, perhaps you would have been able to detect, to find out that it was a mirage. You have seen mirages before; you know that mirages can appear almost as if they are real – but your thirst is there. The physical phenomenon of the returning rays of the sun gives half the reality to the mirage. The other, and the far more important half, is contributed by you and your thirst. You want to believe that it is true. Even if somebody was there trying to prove that it was not real, you would feel angry with this man: you are thirsty and the water is there and he is trying to prove that the water is illusory. He does not know what thirst means – perhaps he is not thirsty. There is no way to convince a thirsty man that what he is seeing is not the real thing.

All that you see is not necessarily real. Appearance does not mean reality. The religions have been saying to people for thousands of years that the happiness in this world is of the same nature as a mirage in the desert. That's why you are never capable of catching hold of it. You never get hold of happiness in your fist; it comes and goes. You can feel it like a breeze, but by the time you become aware that it is here, it is already gone. Perhaps it is more unreal than the mirage. A mirage at least has some reality – the reflected sunrays contribute half and your thirst the other half. But in your so-called happiness of this world, you are contributing one hundred percent; there is nothing else there which contributes anything.

And you know it. Today a woman is so beautiful to you that you can say Cleopatra was nothing before her. She seems to be the most beautiful woman in the world. Not only today – you cannot conceive that there could have been any woman more beautiful ever, or could be in the future. You are projecting, because the same woman to others is nothing, and the same woman tomorrow will be nothing to you, too. Then you will be surprised, shocked – what happened? What happened to the woman? Nothing has happened to the woman, she is the same person; something has happened to you.

Yesterday you were thirsty; lust was being projected. Today the lust is fulfilled; now there is no biological projection. The woman is an ordinary woman, and the happiness that you got was just from your projection – you created the whole game. The woman, at the most, played the part of an inactive participant; she allowed you to project yourself upon her. Perhaps she was also projecting her mind upon you, so it was a projection from both sides. Sooner or later it is going to disappear because projections cannot last once their basic cause is missing.

The basic cause is in your biology; and biology doesn't bother about love and poetry and romance, or anything – biology means business! Biology is not interested in foreplay and afterplay, a sheer wastage; biology is interested in reproduction. Once biology has done its work, it withdraws; the projection disappears. Then you are standing there, the same woman is standing there – but nothing is the same any longer.

Where has the happiness disappeared to? You were feeling like you were on the top of Everest, and you have fallen to the depths of the Pacific. The woman deceived you, and the woman thinks you deceived her, and you both try to dump on each other. Nobody has deceived – both have been deceived by biology. But biology is not somebody outside you; it is intrinsic to your body. You are a projection of two other biologies, those of your father, your mother, and they were a projection of two other biologies. It is a continuum, a river-like flow.

The religions tried to exploit this fundamental truth. It is true that romance and poetry is one thing, but the so-called love affair is just a shadow of biology. So it is not very difficult: a certain injection with certain hormones can create all the poetry right now, all the romance. Another injection, and you fall into the Pacific! Now we know a man can become a woman, a woman can become a man; just a little change of hormones, just a little change of chemistry.

Religions exploited this simple truth. It is true, but rather than explaining it to you, they exploited it. They said, "This is momentary happiness. Don't run after it; you are wasting your time. The real world is beyond death." Why beyond death? Because death will destroy all your biology, physiology, chemistry. Everything that is material, death will take away. Only the spiritual will be left behind, and the spiritual knows the eternal. The material, the physical, knows only the momentary.

It appeared very logical; the first part is true. The second part is fictitious. Yes, it is true that moments of happiness in this life are very fleeting, but that does not mean there is another life beyond death where these moments become eternal. There is no evidence for it. At least these moments are there, are experienced by everyone. Howsoever small and fleeting, they exist. Nobody can deny their existence. You can say they are made of the same stuff as dreams are made of – but still they are there. Even dreams have a reality of their own. They are there, and they affect you; and when something affects you it becomes real.

For example, you are hungry. The whole day you have not been able to eat anything; you are tired, you fall asleep. Now, the body is hungry and wants food. The mind creates a beautiful dream that you are a guest in a great feast. The mind is serving you, because if the mind is not going to create the dream, your sleep will be disturbed. The hunger is there – somehow you have to be convinced that you are eating, that you are not hungry. Your sleep remains undisturbed. The dream is doing something real.

How can something unreal do something real? It is not possible, but a dream has its own existence. Yes, it is different from a rock, but so is a rose flower different from a rock. The dream is even more different; but it affects you, it affects your life, it affects your lifestyle – and those changes are real.

So, one thing to be remembered: in this life there are momentary pleasures, fleeting experiences of happiness, sudden explosions of joy – but you cannot catch hold of them. You cannot keep them in your safe deposit. You cannot make them permanent. Just because you cannot make

> "Yes, it is true that moments of happiness in this life are very fleeting, but that does not mean there is another life beyond death where these moments become eternal."

them permanent, religions have exploited you. It was a very cunning strategy. You want to make them permanent; your deepest desire is to remain happy for ever, not to know pain, sadness, anguish – ever. Just to be always in paradise – that is your desire.

The religions exploited this. They said, "There is such a place, but you cannot get anything without paying for it." It looks perfectly mathematical, economical. The religions started teaching that you have to sacrifice this life if you want to attain the permanent world of paradise that is beyond death. And it is very cheap, because what you are sacrificing are just momentary, once in a while, fleeting experiences.

If you collect all the moments of happiness in the seventy years of your life, perhaps you may not get even seven moments which you can be absolutely certain were of the nature of ecstasy.

In seventy years of life, not even seven moments? Then what have you been doing here – torturing yourself and others? Yes, you cannot find even seven moments, because the nature of those moments is such that when they are there, they take you over totally, they possess you – yes, that is the right word – they possess you completely. But when they are gone, they dispossess you as completely as they had possessed you, so only a memory is left. And how long can you live on the memory which proved so deceptive?

After a few days you start doubting whether it happened or: "Was I just imagining?" Because in your whole life's experience, that moment is so contradictory: years pass, then one moment perhaps… and that too is not in your hands. When and where it is going to happen, you cannot decide. So, years of dragging, and a certain moment that has remained just a memory… Slowly, slowly, even the smoke of memory starts disappearing.

> "For thousands of years they have found the greatest business: they have been selling you paradise, and almost for nothing."

So even if you ask a man who is seventy years old, he cannot say that there were even seven moments. And as you become older, there is less and less possibility of those moments. There is more and more disillusionment, more and more disappointment. In the future there is only death and darkness, and in the past nothing but deception.

The religions had a beautiful space through which to exploit you – and they did well all over the world. For thousands of years they have found the greatest business – greater than anybody else's: they have been selling you paradise, and almost for nothing. All they ask is, "Renounce this momentary life and the eternal world of ecstasy is yours." Hence renunciation became a foundational belief: the more you renounce, the more you become worthy, and the more you can be certain that you are coming closer. So people have tried to renounce everything.

Mahavira was going to be the king. His father was old, and he was continually asking Mahavira, "Now let me retire. I am tired; and you are ready, young, well educated – I am perfectly satisfied. Where can I find a better son than you? Just be ready to relieve me." But Mahavira had other ideas. While he was being educated by the priests and the monks, they had poisoned his mind. They had told him that if he could renounce the kingdom, "Then the kingdom of God is yours." The greater the renunciation the greater, of course, will be the reward. That's why the twenty-four great masters of the Jainas were all kings.

I have been asking the Jaina monks, "What is the secret of this? Was there nobody else in the country who could attain, become a great master – a warrior, a brahmin, a scholar, anybody – why only kings?" They don't have any answer. I used to tell them, "I am not asking you for the answer because I have the answer. I am just asking you the question so that you start thinking about it."

The answer is simple: because they renounced the kingdom, the greatest reward had to be theirs. A poor man can renounce whatsoever he has – but what has he? He cannot become a *tirthankara,* the supreme-most master. Even in paradise he will be living somewhere outside the town. He won't get in because they will ask, "What have you renounced? In the first place what have you got to renounce?" So of course the kings will be very close to the palace of God; then will come the richest, the super-rich people; then the middle class people; then the lowest strata and then will come those who had nothing to renounce – they were already without anything. In fact they should be by the side of God already because they don't have anything. But they will be outside the boundary lines of paradise; they will not be able to show what their bank balance is in the other world.

All the Hindu avatars are kings: Rama, Krishna... Buddha is also a king. It is strange that these people are drawn only from kings, but if you understand the structure, the strategy of the priest, it is clear: they have renounced the most, naturally they are promised the most. Nobody knows whether they got anything after death or not, but the idea became so ingrained for the simple reason that it has a grain of truth in it: in this life everything is momentary.

To me, nothing is wrong if it is momentary. In fact, because it is momentary it is so exciting, so ecstatic. Make it permanent and it will be dead. In the morning, the rose flower opens up, so fresh, with fresh dewdrops still on its petals, so fragrant. You cannot conceive that just by the evening these petals will be falling into dust and the rose will disappear. You would like it to remain permanent, but then you need a plastic flower; a real flower won't do.

A real flower has to be momentary. To be real it has to be momentary; only plastic things can be permanent.

Plastic is a new discovery. It was not known to Buddha, Mahavira, Mohammed, Jesus, but I can say to you that paradise must be made of plastic. If there is any paradise it cannot be anything but plastic, because plastic has the quality of not dying; it is deathless. Now scientists are worried – particularly the environmental-ists are very worried – because plastic is so cheap that you go on disposing of it. Glass was not so cheap; you were saving the bottles or returning the bottles and getting your deposit back. Plastic is so cheap that everything made of plastic is disposable: use it once and dispose of it. But you don't know where it is going. It is getting collected in the oceans, in the riverbeds, in the lakes under the earth, and there is no way for nature to dissolve it because nature is not prepared, was not made to absorb plastic.

> *"A real flower has to be momentary. To be real it has to be momentary; only plastic things can be permanent."*

If God has made this world, he certainly is not all-knowing. At least one thing he did not know: that plastic was going to happen one day. He has not made anything in nature, any chemicals, which can dissolve plastic. So plastic goes on accumulating. Soon it will have accumulated so much that it will destroy the fertility of the earth, it will poison the waters. Nothing can destroy it; it will destroy everything.

In the Hindu paradise, the *apsaras* – how to translate the word *apsara*? They are call girls for those great sages who live in paradise. Of course, they need call girls. Those call girls, those *apsaras*, are the most beautiful; it has to be so. They remain always young – that gives me the clue that they are plastic. They are stuck at the age of sixteen; for millions of years they remain just sixteen. In the Indian mind, sixteen is the mature age for a woman, so they remain at sixteen.

Apsaras don't perspire; neither Mahavira nor Buddha nor Jesus nor Mohammed had any idea of deodorants, so the only thing they could conceive of was that those girls who serve the sages should not perspire. But only if your body is made of plastic will you not perspire; otherwise, perspiration is absolutely necessary. And those girls will not get old, will not die.

Nothing dies in paradise, nothing gets old, nothing changes; it must be an utterly boring place. Can you imagine the boredom – where everything remains the same every day? There is no need for any newspaper there. I have heard that only once was one newspaper published – one edition, on one day – and it flopped because after that nothing happened! It described everything in the first edition; that was the last edition also.

This desire for permanency is somehow sick; but it was there, so the religious firms – yes, I call them firms – Christian, Hindus, Mohammedans, for centuries did great business. They are still doing it, and their business can never end for the simple reason that they sell invisible commodities. They take visible things from you and they give you invisible things which you have to believe in.

I am reminded of a story. A king had conquered the whole world and he was very restless – now what to do? He was thinking that once he had conquered the whole world he would rest. He had never thought that he would be so restless; he had never been so restless. While fighting, continuously invading, going on and on –

because there is always some place to go, some enemy to destroy, some country to conquer – there was no space, no time to be restless, he was so occupied. But now he had conquered the whole world, he was utterly restless – what to do now?

A con man heard about this situation. He came to the palace, asked for an audience with the king, and said, "I have the remedy for restlessness."

Immediately he was taken inside, because all the physicians had failed. The king could not sleep, could not sit, was walking back and forth, and was continually worried. He was asking, "What to do now? Isn't there another world? Find out! We will conquer it."

This con man came into the court before the king, and he said, "Don't be worried. You are the first man who has conquered the whole world. You are worthy to receive the clothes of God himself – and I can manage it."

This was a great idea. The king became immediately interested. He said, "Start working! God's own clothes… Have they ever before come on the earth?"

The man said, "Never, because nobody has been worthy of them. You are the first man. So for the first time, I will bring the clothes from paradise for you."

The king said, "Every preparation should be made. How much will it cost?"

The man said, "They are beyond cost; still, millions of rupees will be needed – but it is nothing."

The king said, "Don't be worried, money is not a problem at all. But don't try to deceive me."

The man said, "There is no question of deception. I will be staying in your palace and you can put your army around the palace. I will be working here; of course, my room has not to be opened until I give a knock from the inside. You can lock it from the outside so you can be completely satisfied that I cannot escape. But whatever money I ask, you have to go on sending to the person whose name I give you. It will take not more than three weeks." And in three weeks he withdrew millions of rupees. He was sending a name every day:

morning, afternoon, night… "Immediately! Urgent!"

The king knew that the work was such… And the man could not deceive him. Where could he go? He was locked in. And certainly he didn't escape. After three weeks the man knocked on the door from the inside, and the door was opened. He came out with a huge, beautiful box. He had gone into the room with the box, saying, "I will have to take the box with me for the clothes I have to bring you." Not to be deceived, the king had opened the box to see whether he was carrying some clothes in it. It was empty, there was no deception, so the box was given back to him.

Now the con man came out and said, "The box will be opened in the court before all the wise, the learned, the generals, the queen, the king, the prince, the princess – everybody has to be present because this is a unique occasion." The man must have been really courageous – con men always are.

When the whole court had assembled, he called the king, "Come close, here. I will open the box. Give me your turban. I will put it in the box, because this is how I have been instructed: first I put your turban in, then take out the turban which God has given, and give it to you. You put it on yourself.

"One thing more," he declared to the court, "these clothes are divine, so only those who are born really from their own fathers will be able to see them. Those who are bastards will miss out. I cannot do anything, this is the condition."

But everybody said, "There is no problem with it. We are born of our fathers."

The king's turban went in, and the con man's empty hand came out, and he said to the king, "Look at the beauty of the turban!" His hand was empty but the whole court started clapping, and everybody was trying to outdo the other, shouting that such a beautiful thing had never been seen.

Now the king thought, "If I say his hand is empty then I am the only bastard and all these bastards are really born of their fathers. So it is better to keep quiet."

In fact, this was the situation with everybody. They all saw his hand was empty, but who would come out and be condemned

when everybody else was seeing something there? They started sus-
pecting, "Perhaps I am a bastard, so better keep quiet. What is the
point of becoming unnecessarily condemned by all the people?" So
they started shouting more loudly in praise of its beauty.

The king put the turban, which was not there, on his head. But
it was not only the turban; by and by, other clothes started disappearing. At last, only his underwear was left. The king thought for a
moment: "Now what to do?" But it was too late to turn back. "If I
have seen the turban and I have seen the coat and I have seen the
shirt, then why can't I see the underwear? Now it is better to see it.
There is no way to go back. This man…"

The man was holding the invisible underwear in his hands, and
was showing them: "Look how many diamonds are on the underwear!"

The whole court was applauding, saying, "Such an experience
has never happened in the whole history of man."

The king's underwear also went in. But that con man was something! He said, "When I was coming, God said to me, 'These clothes
are going into the world for the first time,
so tell the king from me that when he
wears these clothes he has to go in a procession round the whole capital, so all
the people can see. Otherwise, those poor
people will never be able to see them.' The
chariot is ready, please come on."

Now, with each step it was difficult to
go back. The king started thinking, "It
would have been better if I had stopped the
whole thing with the turban – but now it is
too late. If I say I am naked…but the whole court is applauding."

*"With invisible
commodities it is
very easy to
exploit people, to
force them to do
things against
themselves."*

And they started saying, "Yes sir, this is right; if God has asked,
it has to be done. And that is the right welcome for the clothes."

The streets were packed with people because the rumor had
gone far and wide that God's clothes were coming. And the king
agreed. Naked, he stood on his chariot, and before him the man was
announcing, "These clothes will be seen only by those who are born
of their own fathers."

So everybody saw them, except a small child who had come with his father. Sitting on his father's shoulders, he said, "Da" – Da means daddy – "the king appears to be naked."

His father said, "You idiot, keep quiet! When you grow up, then you will be able to see those clothes. It needs a certain maturity; only a child like you cannot see the clothes. Keep quiet if you want to see. I was not willing from the very beginning to bring you here."

But the child could not resist; again and again he said, "But I see him clearly, naked." The father had to escape with the child out of the crowd, because if others heard him it would have meant that the child was not his but somebody else's.

With invisible commodities it is very easy to exploit people, to force them to do things against themselves – and that's what renunciation is. It is conmanship, done by the priest in the name of God, truth, *moksha*, nirvana. Their names may be different, but the priest is the greatest con man in the world. Other conmen are just small criminals. Of what can they cheat you? But the priest, the prophet, the messiah, the avatar, the *tirthankara* – these are the super conmen. They have sold things which nobody has seen, which nobody is ever going to see. Not a single witness exists. Nobody has returned from death and said, "Yes, there is eternal beauty, eternal joy, eternal silence, eternal peace." The business goes on because nobody can contradict it. If you contradict it you are wrong, because the whole world believes in it.

But there was a certain truth which they tried to fix into their strategy of exploitation: in life everything is momentary. Nothing is wrong in it; it has to be so. If it were otherwise, life would have been intolerable. Things change, and it is good that they change; otherwise they would be dead. Change keeps them alive.

You are changing continuously. Do you remember on what day you jumped from childhood and became a young man, or when from youth you became an old man? You cannot draw the line between when you were a child, when you were adolescent, when you became a young man, when you became middle-aged, when you became old. Can you draw the line? No, every moment you are changing; it is an ongoing process. Since you were conceived, you have been changing. In the mother's womb, in those nine months you changed so much; in ninety years of your life you will not change so much. If you are shown pictures of the nine months' life in your mother's womb you will not recognize that they are your pictures. Or do you think that you can recognize them? You have changed completely, and you are changing every moment – and not only you; everything around you is changing. All the stars are moving and changing. Every day some star dies and disappears – it may have been here for millions of years – another star is born. Every day that is going on.

> *"Life is a flux, a movement, a continuum. There is nothing wrong in it. Enjoy that moment which comes and goes."*

Life is a flux, a movement, a continuum. There is nothing wrong in it. Enjoy that moment which comes and goes. Drink out of it as much as you can, because it is fleeting – so don't waste time thinking. Don't start thinking that it is fleeting. Don't be bothered about what will happen tomorrow, whether this will be with you or not; and don't think of yesterdays. While it lasts, squeeze the whole juice out of it, drink of it completely. Then who cares whether it goes away or if it remains? If it remains, we will be drinking it. If it goes, good, we will be drinking some other moment.

Why should you insist that this moment remain permanent? How do you know that better moments are not coming? Just a moment before, you would not have thought of this moment. And who knows – when this moment goes, something better may be on the way. In fact, it is on the way, because if you have drowned yourself in this moment totally, you have learned something of tremendous importance. You will be using that in the coming moment.

Each moment your maturity is growing. Each moment you are becoming more and more centered, more and more in the moment, more and more aware, more and more alert, more and more capable of living. So who cares about death? We will enjoy it when we die. Death will also be a moment in life. Death is not the end of life, but only a moment of transformation, because nothing can die. You cannot destroy anything; it only changes shapes, forms.

Now science is capable of destroying Hiroshima, Nagasaki, the whole world – but not really. It cannot destroy a single piece of stone. It cannot destroy it totally, it cannot annihilate it; it will still be there. You can break it into pieces but those pieces will be there. You can heat it as much as if you have brought the sun itself under it; it will melt, but it will be there. Yes, you can change the form, but there is no way to throw it out of existence.

Nothing dies, nothing is born.

Birth simply means that the form that you were was not this form, but some other form, so you cannot recognize it. You cannot even recognize pictures of you in your mother's womb. If I show you a picture of your past life, are you going to recognize it? Forget about the mother's womb, you may not be able to recognize the picture of when you were three months old, six months old, nine months old. Continuously, everything goes on changing.

Death is a great transformation.

You ask what the place of renunciation in my religion is. Before I answer you, there is one thing more to be noted: this idea of renunciation became so deep-rooted in the whole of humanity that even the people who have denied the existence of life after death have also used the same logic. The logic became almost universal.

For example, in India there was a school of atheists called the Charvakas. The word *charvaka* is worth understanding. Their enemies – and all the religions are enemies of Charvakas – have burned all the books, so not a single book of the Charvakas is available. All that we know is from the scriptures of Hindus, Jainas, and Buddhists criticizing the Charvakas. So we can guess something of what those people were saying, but we cannot be absolutely certain. And these are all religious people, and they destroyed the Charvakas' scriptures. Perhaps they have killed many of them also, because today there is not a single Charvaka in India. And all the scriptures are so much against the Charvakas that it seems they must have once been a tremendous force. Otherwise why criticize them when there is nobody who follows the philosophy?

All three religions were continually hammering and arguing against the Charvakas. It must have been a very popular philosophy. And in fact, it is still a powerful philosophy all over the world – but because people are hypocrites, they don't recognize it. Just listen to their philosophy and you will see that out of one hundred people, ninety-nine point nine percent are Charvakas. They may be Christians, they may be Hindus, they may be Mohammedans, it doesn't matter; these are just masks.

So the enemy scriptures describe the meaning of the word *charvaka*: eat, drink, and be merry. Charvaka means one who believes in eating, eating, eating – through all the senses. I cannot say that any Charvakas have said it, but it is possible. The enemy scriptures quote Charvakas as saying, "Even if you have to borrow money, don't be worried, but drink, eat, be merry. Go on borrowing money because after death neither are you there to pay, nor is there anybody else to ask you, 'What about my money?' Everything is finished with death, so don't be bothered by these priests telling you that you will suffer for your karmas. Enjoy yourself in every possible way. Don't miss enjoyment. This is the only world."

This is the meaning given by the enemies, but in one enemy scripture – it must have been a very liberal person who wrote it – it says that this is the meaning given by the enemies, by us. But Charvakas themselves have a different meaning of their name. It means one who has a sweet philosophy – that meaning is possible from the same word – one who speaks words of honey. And certainly they do speak words of honey. But they also are trapped in the same logic.

The religious people say, "Renounce this world if you want to enjoy that world." And Charvakas say, "Renounce that world if you want to rejoice in this one." But the logic is the same. They have taken it from different angles, but both are asking you to renounce one for the other. Charvakas say renounce the other world; there is no God, no nirvana, no paradise – renounce it. This is all there is, so enjoy it.

In Greece, Epicurus had the same philosophy and got caught up in the same logic. Even Karl Marx was caught up in the same logic:

there is no other world. The first effort is to deny the other world, only then can you enjoy this world. So first demolish the other world: there is no God, no paradise, no heaven, nothing. There is no soul to survive; with your body everything dies. You are nothing but your body, your chemistry, your biology, your physiology, all together – a by-product of all these things. It is just like a clock that goes on working – it does not mean there is a soul which is moving the hands. Just take the pieces apart and you won't find any soul, just a certain arrangement of the parts. Arrange it again, and it starts ticking. Karl Marx says, "Consciousness is only a by-product, it has no independent existence." So when the body dies, consciousness disappears.

Why this insistence on denying the other world? – for the simple reason that unless you deny the other, you will not be able to enjoy this.

But please see my point of view, which is totally different from all these people – the religious, the anti-religious, the theist, the atheist. I don't belong to any of them. I say to you that life continues to exist, but there is no need to call

> "Life continues to exist, but there is no need to call it 'the other world.' It is the same world, the same continuity."

it "the other world." It is the same world, the same continuity. The Ganges arises in the Himalayas; it is just a small rivulet. As it descends, other waterfalls, other rivulets go on joining it; it goes on becoming bigger and bigger and bigger. When it comes out of the Himalayas it is a vast river. You cannot conceive that it is the same river. You can see from where it arises. Because Hindus love the cow as the mother, they have made the origin of the Ganges a stone cow's face. The Ganges falls through the face; it is so small, so tiny.

By the time the Ganges reaches Varanasi, you cannot believe its size. And when it reaches, near Kolkata, to meet the ocean, it becomes almost oceanic itself. Standing there, you cannot decide which is the ocean; it is so vast. It falls into the ocean; then too it remains. Where can it go? Yes, it is no longer a river – perhaps some water may evaporate into the clouds, some water may become ice and move toward the arctic – but it will remain, nothing is lost. So I don't say that you have to renounce anything: this world for that, or that world for this. You have not to renounce at all. You have to live! You have to live intensely and totally, wherever you are, whatever you are.

And if you enjoy this time, this space, this opportunity that is available to you, in its totality, you will certainly be moving to a higher consciousness. You will be gaining, learning, understanding, becoming more aware. Life will continue. It will depend on your awareness what form it takes, higher or lower, whether it moves toward more anguish or more ecstasy – but it depends on this moment. So I am not saying to renounce this world.

I am a strange man in a way, because I am against the religions. Religious people in India have been writing against me in books and articles – and Communists have been writing books and articles against me too.

Once I was traveling, and the president of India's Communist Party, S. A. Dange, was also with me in the compartment. His son-in-law had just written a book against me. He asked me, "Have you seen the book my son-in-law has written against you?"

I said, "I am so much involved in living that I don't care who is writing what about me. And anybody who is writing about me must be a fool because he is wasting his time writing about me. He should live! Or even if he wants to write, he should write something about himself. And why should I read his crap? He may be your son-in-law – so you can read it, I'm not interested."

He was ready to give me the book. I said, "Throw it out of the window, because so many books have been written against me, I cannot waste my time." I told him, "Just for your information, it is strange but religious people write against me and anti-religious people, Communists, also write against me. This has never happened before."

But the reason is that I am trying to give you a totally new viewpoint, which goes against all the old logic. They are both partners in the same game, and I am trying to destroy their whole game, the whole logic.

They both believe that one world has to be renounced; which one is another matter. But on one point they agree: one world has to be renounced. The religions say this for that; the Communists say that for this – that is the only disagreement between them. But the basic logic is similar: you can have only one world. And I say: why can't we have both? I don't see any conflict; I am having both. And my experience is that the more you have of this, the more you will have of that, because you will become more experienced.

If there is a paradise, then one thing is certain: your monks will not be able to enjoy it. What will they enjoy? The whole of their life they were denouncing women, condemning women, and there they will find beautiful call girls. They will be so nervous; many of them will have heart attacks. Here they are renouncing: you should not eat food with taste, taste is an attachment to food – and there they will be served the most tasteful food; they will be vomiting. Their whole life experience will be against it.

> "I do not give you a fixed idea because if I give you a fixed idea, I am your enemy; I make you a fixed person, inflexible, rigid, dead."

Only my people can enjoy paradise fully. Neither the religious people can enjoy it, because they have destroyed and crippled themselves and their capacity to enjoy, nor the Communists, because they will not open their eyes. They have denied the existence of anything after death. They will keep their eyes closed to remain convinced that there is nothing; otherwise their whole life's philosophy is proved wrong. It is better to keep your eyes closed. That's what people do: if anything goes against you, any fact, you try to avoid that fact; it is disturbing. Communists will go blind; they cannot accept the idea that Karl Marx is wrong and *Das Kapital* is wrong. And the religious people will be the most troubled people in paradise, everywhere they will find difficulty. Perhaps there are divisions in paradise, as it seems. Mohammedans' paradise seems to be different from the

Hindus, from the Christians, from the Jainas – perhaps different zones are allotted to different kinds of people.

Only my people will be able to swim in any zone. They will fit anywhere because they haven't any fixed routine of living, a fixed style of living. All that I am teaching them is to remain flexible, free, open, available to new experiences, to new explorations. So my people are not going to remain in one zone. They are going to use all the zones and enjoy all the sights of paradise; nobody can prevent them.

You can have both worlds – so why cripple people? Make this life an experience, a school, a learning, a discipline, because something unknown is going to open up after death and you have to be ready in every possible way. Don't miss any opportunity of living. Who knows what kind of life you are going to have after death?

I do not give you a fixed idea because if I give you a fixed idea, I am your enemy; I make you a fixed person, inflexible, rigid, dead. Be flexible, so you can move in any dimension that becomes available.

In my religion there is no place for renunciation.

The Sanskrit word for renunciation is *sannyas,* because renunciation became so important that the very word *sannyas* was used for it. But I have given it a new meaning. The people who have called sannyas renunciation, meant by sannyas "the right way of renouncing life." By sannyas I mean "the right way of living life."

The word *sannyas* can mean both. When it can mean the right way of living, why cripple people, cut off their life, destroy their naturalness, their spontaneity? Why not help them to have as many aspects to their life as possible, as many dimensions open to them as possible? My sannyasin is multidimensional. The whole of life is yours. Love it, live it to the fullest. That's the only way to get ready for death.

Then you can live death too, to its fullest; and it is one of the most beautiful experiences. There is nothing comparable to the death experience in life, except deep meditation.

So those who know meditation know something of death – that's the only way to know before dying.

If I am saying there is no more significant experience in life than death, I am saying it not because I have died and come back to tell you, but because I know that in meditation you move into the same space as death – because in meditation you are no longer your physiology, no longer your biology, no longer your chemistry, no longer your psychology. All these are left far away. You come to your innermost center where there is only pure awareness. That pure awareness will be with you when you die because that cannot be taken away. All those things which can be taken away, we take away with our own hands in meditation. So meditation is an experience of death in life. And it is so beautiful, so indescribably beautiful that only one thing can be said about death: it must be that experience multiplied by millions. The experience of meditation multiplied by millions is the experience of death.

And when you pass on you simply leave your form behind. You are absolutely intact, and for the first time out of the prison of physiology, biology, psychology. All the walls are broken and you are free. For the first time you can open your wings to the existential.

CHAPTER 2

The Worst Profession in the World

Bertrand Russell, in his autobiography, has a very profound statement. He says, "If misery in the world ends, all the religions will end of their own accord. It is misery that is keeping religions alive." He is speaking from a very different angle. He was an atheist; he wanted all religions to disappear.

I am not an atheist. I also want all the religions to disappear, but for a different reason. He wants religions to disappear because he thinks religions have been detrimental to the evolution of man. I want religions to disappear so that religiousness can have the whole space that is being occupied by religions. Religions have been detrimental to the progress of religiousness, and to me, religiousness is the highest flower of evolution.

The very existence of three hundred religions on the earth indicates definitely that man has missed understanding the very spirit of religion. There cannot be three hundred chemistries – not even three – there cannot be three hundred mathematics. About the objective world, we are so clear that science is one, and can only be one, without any adjective attached to it.

It would look so stupid to say Hindu science, Mohammedan science, Christian physics, Jaina mathematics. But that's what has happened with religion. And religion is your very soul, your very interiority, your very subjectivity. How is it possible that there can be so many religions? There can be only one religiousness. I will not even call it a religion for the simple reason that the moment you use a noun, growth has stopped. "Religion" means something has come to a stop. "Religiousness" means something continuously growing, flowering, bringing new spaces and new secrets unrevealed to you, undreamed of.

Religion is the very river of existence. It knows no beginning, it knows no end.

> *"I am not an atheist. I also want all the religions to disappear, but for a different reason."*

What you have known up to now in the name of religion is nothing more than self-hypnosis. Real religion is becoming free from all hypnosis. Then God is not a person, then God is the whole, then God is the sum total of this whole existence. Then an amazing stream of juices flows because wherever you go, you meet the divine. Then this world, this life is very beautiful. When life becomes so beautiful, know that religiousness has arisen in your life; it has commenced, the first drop of religiousness has fallen.

An ancient story: A young devil comes running to his boss. He is trembling, and he says to the old devil, "Something has to be done immediately because on the earth, a man has found the truth! And once people know the truth, what will happen to our profession?"

The old man laughed and he said, "Sit down and rest and don't be worried. Everything is taken care of. Our people have reached there."

"But," the young devil said, "I am coming from there, and I have not seen a single devil."

The old man said, "The priests are my people! They have already surrounded the man who has found the truth. Now they will become the mediators between the man of truth and the masses. They will raise temples, they will write scriptures, they will interpret and distort everything. They will ask people to worship, to pray. And in all this hubbub, the truth will be lost. This is my old method, which has always succeeded."

The priests who represent religion are not its friends. They are the greatest enemies of it, because religion needs no mediators: between you and existence there is an immediate relatedness. All that you have to learn is how to understand the language of existence. You know the languages of man, but they are not the languages of existence.

Existence knows only one language, and that is of silence.

> "Existence knows only one language, and that is of silence."

If you can also be silent you will be able to understand the truth, the meaning of life, the significance of all that exists. And there is no one who can interpret it for you. Everyone has to find it for himself. Nobody can do the job on your behalf – but that's what the priests have been doing for centuries. They are standing like a Wall of China between you and existence.

If people start approaching reality without anybody leading them, without anybody telling them what is good and what is evil, without anybody giving them a map that they have to follow, millions of people will be able to understand existence – because our heartbeat is also the heartbeat of the universe, our life is part of the life of the total.

We are not strangers, we are not coming from somewhere else; we are growing within existence. We are part of it, an essential part of it. We just have to be silent enough, so that we can hear that which cannot be said in words: the music of existence, the immense joy of existence, the constant celebration of existence. Once it starts penetrating our heart, transformation comes.

That is the only way somebody becomes religious – not by going to the churches, which are made by man; not by reading the scriptures, which are made by man.

But the priests have been pretending that their holy scriptures are written by God. The very idea is simply idiotic. Just look into those scriptures: you will not find any signature of God in them. You will find things that there is no reason for God to write. Hindus believe in the Vedas and believe that they are written by God himself, and they are the most ancient books in existence; but no Hindu bothers to look into them. If God wrote them, there is going to be something immensely valuable...but ninety-eight percent of the Vedas are just rubbish – such rubbish that it proves that they are not written by God.

For example, a prayer by a priest... Why should God write it? The prayer is that his cows are not giving enough milk, "Have mercy on me, increase the milk of my cows." Not only that, "Decrease the milk of everybody else's!"

God is going to write this? "Kill my enemies and help my friends," and even such stupid things as "The rains are coming; take care that all the water reaches my fields and avoids the neighboring field, because it belongs to my enemy. Just shower your water on my field."

Why should God write these things?

Every scripture gives intrinsic evidence that it is written by men – and very stupid men, primitive men. The so-called holy scriptures are not even to be counted as good literature – they are childish, crude, ugly. But because they are written in languages that are dead... And some are in languages which have never been in use by common people, for example, the Vedas. That language has never been used by the common people. It was the language of the learned brahmins, the language of the priests, and they were very reluctant that it should be translated because they knew: once it is translated, it will lose all sanctity. People will see that this nonsense is not even unholy, what to say about its being holy!

The scriptures are man-made, the statues of God are man-made, the temples and churches are man-made, but thousands of years of conditioning have given them a certain sacredness, holiness. And there is nothing sacred in them, nothing holy in them.

The priests have been deceiving man more than anybody else. This is the worst profession in the world, even worse than the profession of the prostitutes. At least the prostitute gives you something in return; the priest gives you simply hot air – he has nothing to give to you.

And this is not all. Whenever somebody has realized the truth, these priests are against him. Obviously they have to be, because if his truth is recognized by people, millions of priests in the world will be out of employment. And their employment is absolutely unproductive. They are parasites, they go on sucking the blood of man. From the moment the child is born until he enters his grave, the priest goes on finding ways to exploit him.

Unless religion is freed from the hands of the priests, the world will remain only with pseudo-religion; it will never become religious. And a religious world cannot be so miserable: the religious world should be a constant celebration. A religious man is nothing but pure ecstasy. His heart is full of songs, his whole being is ready to dance any moment.

But the priest has taken away the search for truth. He says there is no need for searching, it has already been found; you just have to have faith.

The priest has made people miserable because he condemns all the pleasures of the world. He condemns the pleasures of the world so that he can praise the pleasures of the other world. The other world is his fiction. And he wants humanity to sacrifice its reality for a fictitious idea – and people have sacrificed.

> "The priests have been deceiving man more than anybody else."

The priests are enemies of everyone who loves truth, who is in search of truth or who has found the truth. The closer you are to the truth, the more the priest is your enemy. You are disturbing his customers, you are disturbing his business. Religion to him is business.

The Christian churches in America were against me for the simple reason that so many young men and women have come out of their fold. My people don't belong to any religion. They are religious, and to be religious you don't have to belong to any religion. Religiousness is a quality, a fragrance of your consciousness. It has nothing to do with belonging to an organization, following fixed and dead principles decided by people who have been long, long dead.

To look at it differently, in the name of religion the dead are dominating the living: they are dictating to you how you should live. They don't know anything about the vast changes that have happened since they died. We are living in a totally different world, in a totally different time, and we need a spontaneous awareness every day to respond to reality. We go on failing because our response is not spontaneous – the reality is new, and our response is thousands of years old. Our failure is absolutely certain. And that constant failure brings misery in life.

> "In the name of religion the dead are dominating the living: they are dictating to you how you should live."

The whole humanity is one, but the priests will not allow it to happen; because if the whole humanity becomes one, drops these adjectives of being a Christian or a Jew or a Hindu or a Mohammedan, the priests will be at a loss. They have a very well-paid profession and they are doing nothing except creating trouble, riots among different religions.

Even coming in contact with them you will be defiled. They are the most ugly and disgusting profession on the earth.

Much of my Catholic mind has been tense with struggle for power, approval, love, sex. Meditation stirs up frustration. What is "just looking"?

Mind, any kind of mind – Catholic or Communist, Jew or Jaina – is the same. Mind is a disease, and every mind creates a prison around you. There are different kinds of prisons; their architecture is different, they are made of different material. Some are made of stones, some are made of bricks, some are made of wood, and so on and so forth, but it does not matter. The material is not important –

you are imprisoned. A Catholic mind has different concepts, a Hindu mind is rooted in a different ideology, but every mind needs an ideology. Even the atheist lives in a prison although he does not believe in God. He thinks he is a disbeliever – he is not. His disbelief is his belief. He fanatically disbelieves, in the same fanatical way that believers believe, sometimes even more fanatically because the people who believe in God remember God only once in a while, maybe on Sundays – it is a Sunday religion – but the atheist continuously argues against God. He remembers God continuously.

There is a very beautiful story in Indian scriptures:

When Narada, a devotee, a great devotee, was dying, God appeared to him. Such things used to happen in the past. They don't happen anymore. And God asked him what he would like, if he had any desire to be fulfilled in the next life. He said, "Yes, I want to be born an atheist."

Even God was puzzled. Remember, such things used to happen in the past; now they no longer happen. God said, "What? You want to be an atheist? Such a great devotee, such a believer, such a religious man who has been singing and singing my name?"

Narada said, "Yes, because although I am a devotee I continuously go on forgetting you. But I have seen atheists who never forget you. That's why I want to be an atheist next time, so that I can remember you continuously. I don't want to forget you even for a single moment. Now you are only one of the items of my mind, but for the atheist you seem to be his whole heart – although he denies you, he remembers you. So just give me one blessing, that I should be born an atheist so that I can talk about you continuously."

> "The creed of the fanatic is: 'We are right, and don't be distracted by the facts – whatsoever the facts say they are bound to be wrong.' The fanatic's creed is, 'We have already concluded what is true. Now the facts have to fit with our creed, not vice versa.'"

This story is beautiful. It says in a very symbolic way that the atheist and the theist are not in different boats.

The Communist goes on arguing against God. Now he has no business with God, nothing to do with God. How was Karl Marx concerned with God? God does not come into it as far as economics is concerned, he is not an economic theory or anything. But Marx was obsessed, continuously obsessed. Again and again he came to deny God, as if God were haunting him.

These are all fanatics. Believers, nonbelievers, Hindus, Mohammedans, Christians – all are fanatics. And the fanatic never looks at the facts; that's why he is a fanatic. The creed of the fanatic is: "We are right, and don't be distracted by the facts – whatsoever the facts say they are bound to be wrong." The fanatic's creed is, "We have already concluded what is true. Now the facts have to fit with our creed, not vice versa."

All these so-called ideologies have created very crippled people. Of course the Catholic mind is one of the most crippled and paralyzed minds in the world because it is repressive – and whenever you repress something you grow ugly. Whatsoever is repressed remains there. Not only does it remain there, it becomes more and more powerful every day. It accumulates energy. If you express it, it evaporates.

For example, a man who gets angry in an ordinary way, just as everybody else does – if you insult him, he gets angry – is not a dangerous person because he will never accumulate so much anger that he can prove dangerous. But a man who goes on repressing his anger is sitting on a volcano. Any day the volcano can erupt; either he is going to commit suicide or murder – less than that won't do.

It is because of repressive religions that so much pornography exists in the world. Pornography exists because of the priests, not because of the *Playboys*. In fact, the *Playboys* are only by-products of the priests. So much pornography exists

> *"Killing arises only if sex is very repressed."*

simply because so much sex has been repressed; it wants to find some way, some outlet. And once you repress sex, it starts finding perverted ways. It can become a political trip – it is sexuality, nothing else, repressed sexuality. That's why in all the armies of the world, sex is repressed. And American soldiers have been continuously in difficulty for the simple reason that it is the first time that any army has been allowed some sexual outlet. American soldiers cannot win; their defeat is certain. Whatsoever they do, wherever they go, they will be defeated for the simple reason that American soldiers are a new phenomenon in the world – they are not sexually repressive. They can't win against the Russians – they could not even win against the Vietnamese. The poor Vietnamese defeated one of the greatest world powers that has ever existed in the

> *"Pornography exists simply because so much sex has been repressed; it wants to find some way, some outlet."*

whole history of man for the simple reason that, if sex is repressed, a man is very dangerous, really dangerous – he is boiling within. He wants to hit hard, he wants to be violent. And the person who is sexually satisfied is not really interested in killing. In fact, all the surveys of American armies show that at least thirty percent of the soldiers did not use their weapons in the war; thirty percent is a big percentage! And if thirty percent of soldiers are not using their weapons at all, they simply go every day to the front and come back without killing anybody, how are they going to win? They are not interested in killing, there is no desire to kill.

Killing arises only if sex is very repressed. It is a strange fact that whenever a society has been affluent, rich, sexually free, it was destroyed by poor, backward, repressive societies. That was the fate of Greek civilization; that was the fate of Roman civilization, that was the fate of the Hindu civilization, and that is going to be the fate of the American civilization. It is very strange that the further evolved a society is, the more vulnerable it is to being destroyed easily by the less evolved, because the less evolved are more repressive – they are more foolish, they are more stupid; they still go on listening to the priests.

These are the foolish people, but these foolish people are dangerous people. They can defeat anybody because they will repress sexuality so much, so much energy will be repressed that it will be ready to explode. Any excuse will be enough.

These are the people who are responsible for all the rapes in the world. This is the experience of my woman sannyasins in India. They love me so much, that's why they are here and suffering so much. It is really a sacrifice to be here, because wherever they go they will be watched by the so-called cultured, religious Hindus with such greedy eyes, as if these people are just there to tear them apart. And whenever they have any chance they hit them, they push them, they do anything ugly that they can do. Women have been molested, raped. And these are the great Hindus, the great religious people, the great spiritual people of the world! But it is natural; I don't see any contradiction. This is repression – any chance and it surfaces.

You ask me, "Much of my Catholic mind has been tense…" It can't be otherwise. You will have to drop it, root and all. You cannot save anything of it. Don't try to save anything of it because it is all contaminated. You say: "It is tense with struggle for power…" It is bound to be. If sex is repressed, it starts moving into other dimensions. It becomes a great lust for power. If sex is repressed, you start asking for approval; that is a poor substitute for love, for appreciation. And now that you are here, you are becoming aware that there is a great need for love, but you are afraid – your Catholic mind is against love. The Catholic mind says, "Love only God."

> *"If sex is repressed, it starts moving into other dimensions. It becomes a great lust for power. If sex is repressed, you start asking for approval; that is a poor substitute for love, for appreciation."*

Now, how can you love God? That is sheer nonsense. You have to love human beings; that is the only way to love God. Love unconditionally, love without any demands. But you have to love the people that surround you – these are God's available forms; you cannot love the formless. "Love God," they say, "and avoid man." Now they are teaching nuns, "Love Christ," and nuns are called "brides of Christ." What nonsense! The poor man was never married, and now so many nuns are married to him, "brides of Christ." Then of course they start imagining, projecting, and then their mind starts playing tricks on them. If you look into the history of monasteries and nunneries in the Middle Ages, you will be surprised. Thousands of cases are on record that nuns were raped by the Devil and his disciples; not only that, nuns even used to become falsely pregnant. What imagination! When a woman imagines, she can imagine far-out things. Men are not that capable of imagining, but women can really imagine things. Women confessed in the courts. And what were these courts doing? These courts consisted of bishops, archbishops, popes. These courts were inquiring about details; in fact they were enjoying as much as possible the details of how the Devil made love to the nuns. If you go into the details you will find them more pornographic, more obscene than anything ever written. These nuns had to confess, and they confessed strange things: that the Devil came in the night and made love to them, and they were absolutely unable, incapable…they could not do anything else. What could they do when the Devil came and took possession of them?

All kinds of sexual perversions arose out of the monasteries. Sex would never have become perverted if it were not for the monasteries and nunneries. And the whole world is dominated by some kind of repression or other.

You have to drop this whole mind. You say: "Meditation stirs up frustration." It will stir up frustration. It is nothing to do with meditation; meditation simply brings your reality to you, and that encounter is frustrating. Seeing the ugliness of your own mind you feel frustrated. But don't be worried. Meditation is bringing up all that is repressed in you; you will have to pass through it. If you know what is there, it can be dropped; if you don't know, how can you drop it? Before something can be dropped it has to be known, well understood. In fact, to understand it perfectly is the only way to drop it.

And the day you drop your mind in toto, you are freed from the priests. Priests are the most cunning people in the world and the most foolish too, because only foolish people are cunning. Intelligent people are never cunning. They need not be cunning – intelligence is enough. When you are not intelligent you have to be cunning as a substitute; you have to learn the ways of cunningness.

But remember, all these priests – Catholic or Protestant, Hindu or Mohammedan – and all these pundits are stupid people, but they have dominated humanity and they have reduced the whole of humanity to a big mass of stupidity. Get out of it!

> *"Meditation is bound to stir up all this that has been done to you for centuries, but that cannot be avoided."*

Meditation is bound to stir up all this that has been done to you for centuries, but that cannot be avoided. If you want to avoid it you will remain the same. You will have to go through this pain of seeing all these ugly things that are in you. But better to see and go through it to reach your innermost core, so that you can find your own intrinsic intelligence, so that you can find your own lost consciousness.

Once freed from the priests you are free from stupidity. Then you are neither Catholic nor Christian nor Hindu nor Mohammedan. Then you are simply a human being, and then great beauty arises in you.

A Catholic priest went into a pet shop to buy a parrot. He was shown an especially fine one which he liked the look of, but he was puzzled by the two strings which were tied to its feet.

"What are they for?" he asked the pet shop manager.

"Ah well, father," came the reply, "that's a very unusual feature of this particular parrot. You see, he is a trained parrot, father – used to be in a circus. If you pull the string on his left foot he says 'Hello,' and if you pull the string on his right foot he says 'Goodbye.'"

"And what happens if I pull both the strings at the same time?"

"I fall off me perch, you fool!" screeched the parrot.

Even parrots are far more intelligent than your priests, than your politicians, than the people who have been dominating you.

Get rid of them. Meditation is a process of getting rid of the whole past, of getting rid of all diseases, of getting rid of all the pus that has gathered in you. It is painful, but it is cleansing, and there is no other way to cleanse you.

Why is the world so sick today? Why are misery and tension increasing?

The sickness of the world today, its increasing misery and tension, is the outcome of all the idiotic ideas that have dominated humanity in the past. It was bound to happen – all the religions are responsible for it. What they have done, whether knowingly or unknowingly, is the cause of the misery, suffering, anguish of the whole of humanity.

Let us think of the most fundamental causes one by one.

The first: All the religions have been imposing the idea that God has created the world and God is omniscient, omnipotent, omnipresent. He knows all, he is all-powerful, he is everywhere. This idea prevented man from doing anything to life to make it better, beautiful. When somebody all-knowing, all-powerful, every-where-present, is looking after the world, then what can *you* do? How far can you see? What can be your contribution? If God is the creator of the world, you cannot improve upon it. If you do anything you can only harm it. You cannot inform it; you cannot be wiser than God.

This idea is one of the most basic causes of the whole anguish through which humanity is passing, and perhaps may perish in. Just think: the way I see it, there is no God who is creating the world, who is looking after the world. Don't throw this responsibility onto someone who doesn't exist. It is *we* who are here – in every way responsible – to make or mar the opportunity. Remove God and put man in his place, and you will have a totally different world.

> "All the religions have been teaching you to shirk your responsibility: 'Throw it onto God!' And there is no God."

The suffering is absolutely unwanted; the anguish is our stupidity. Man can live a tremendously rich, blissful, ecstatic life. But the first thing is, he has to accept his responsibility.

All the religions have been teaching you to shirk your responsibility: "Throw it onto God!" And there is no God. You don't do anything because you think God is going to do everything – and there is no God to do anything. Then what else can you expect? What is happening and has happened and is going to happen is the natural outcome of this idea of a creator.

If man were told, "This is your existence; you are responsible whatever you are, whatever you do, and whatever happens around you. Be mature. Don't remain childish"... But this God does not allow you to mature. His "god-ness" depends on your immaturity, on your childishness. The more stupid you are, the more gullible you are, the greater is God. The more intelligent you are, the less is God. If you are really intelligent there is no God. Then this existence is there, you are there – then create! But "the Creator" does not allow *you* to become the creator.

My whole approach is that you are to become the creator. You have to release your creative energies. And this is possible only if this God, who is nothing but a Godot, is removed, absolutely removed, from your vision of life. Yes, in the beginning you will feel very empty because that place of God in you has been filled: for millions of years he was there; the sacred shrine in your heart was filled with the idea of God. Now, suddenly throwing it out, you will feel empty, afraid, lost. But it is good to feel empty. It is good to feel afraid. It is good to be lost because this is the reality, and what you were feeling before was only fiction. Fictions cannot help much; they may give you some consolation, but consolation is not a good thing.

What is needed is transformation, not consolation. What is needed is treatment of all the diseases that you have been carrying, not consolation. So the first thing is: remove God. Don't wait for any Godot. There is none. There has never been any.

Friedrich Nietzsche said... I disagree with him, but my disagreement is totally different from the disagreement of others who disagree. Nietzsche says, "God is dead." Of course Christians have differed, Mohammedans have differed, Hindus have differed, Buddhists have differed – everybody has been against Friedrich Nietzsche. I am also against him, but my reason for differing is that God is not dead because he has never been alive. Even to say "God is dead" is to accept that he was there and now he is no more. No – he was never there in the first place! Man has lived under a fiction.

And this situation, this misery, this increasing tension… The tension is so much that now in the most advanced countries, the second greatest factor causing death is not a disease but suicide. One feels so utterly tense, day after day, and there seems to be no way out. The anguish goes on increasing, and one cannot even see the reason. For what are we suffering? Why should we be suffering, what have we done? Life itself seems to be worthless.

A point comes in the intelligent man's life when he sees it is all futile, meaningless. Then why go on dragging? Why not finish it, why not get rid of it? It has not given you anything except pain; it is not going to give you anything else except pain. Yes, there is an opium somewhere, the hope: "Perhaps tomorrow things may be different." Perhaps if not today, tomorrow you may be able to get some moment of bliss. But even then it does not seem to be worth it. Such a long caravan of miseries and then once in a while, a moment when you can smile, laugh. And by the time you have smiled it is gone. Perhaps that moment is also your imagination. Just to keep yourself going you start dreaming of things that are not really there; you only *wanted* them to be there.

That's actually the function of dreaming. Do you know? It has been a strange discovery of modern psychology. For centuries we thought that dreams are useless, just a disturbance in the night. To have a dreamless sleep has been thought a healthy goal. For ten thousand years Yoga has been teaching that dreamless sleep is the most beautiful experience. But what we have found recently goes against this whole thing. You can drop your dreamless moments of sleep without any harm to you, but you cannot drop your dreams.

If you sleep eight hours, then almost two hours you have sleep without dreams – in fragments, in total two hours – and six hours sleep with dreams. It has been experimented with, now we know. There are instruments which give an indication of whether the person is dreaming or not dreaming. Even without instruments, if you watch his eyelids, you can know immediately. If his eyes are moving inside the lids, he is dreaming – because he is seeing things, movement. If the eyes are static – not moving, and the lids show no movement of the eyes inside – that means dreams have stopped. No sophisticated instruments are needed. But now we have sophisticated instruments which make a graph when the person is dreaming, when the person is not dreaming, just like a cardiogram.

They disturbed a few sleepers when they were dreaming; they would disturb them immediately, they would wake them up. They would allow them only those two hours of nondreaming. In the morning those people were utterly exhausted, listless, with no desire even to live. This was strange, because all the old Yoga tradition in India, in Tibet, in China – different schools and different people not connected with each other at all – have always been saying, "If you can have two hours of dreamless sleep, that is enough nourishment, enough to rejuvenate you." It has not been found true. But if you disturb those two hours when people are not dreaming, and allow them those six hours of dreaming, in the morning they get up so fresh, so young, so rejuvenated, so full of life and juice, and so eager to live.

When for the first time it was discovered, it was a shock. Dreams are absolutely necessary for these people. For what reason? They have not been able to find the reason. They will never be able to find it because that reason can be found only through deep meditation, there is no other way to find it. By psychological experiments they will not be able to find the reason.

But through meditation, something happens that is dreamless, sleepless. Both are not there; neither the dream is there nor is the sleep there. You are fully awake. The body is fast asleep in a deep rest, but your consciousness is absolutely cloudless. There is no sleep. Inside like a flame you are alert, awake, watching –

watching that there is nothing to watch! The body is asleep and there is nothing to watch. But the watcher is. You can only watch the watcher. You can only observe the observer. You can only be aware of your awareness. But there is no sleep, no dream. And in the morning you are as fresh as it is possible to be.

So the psychologists will not be able to understand it; they have not yet been able and will never be able to know unless they start moving toward meditation. And there seems to be no sign of their movement. In fact they are very antagonistic to meditation, and I can understand why. They are antagonistic to meditation because meditation can dissolve all your problems, can dissolve all your psychic anxieties, and with them goes the whole profession of the psychologist.

Just as the priest has been afraid that God should not be doubted, the politician has been afraid that the priest should not be doubted; because if God is doubted, the priest is gone, his priesthood is gone. And there are millions of priests in the world: Hindus, Catholics, Jews, rabbis, ministers, missionaries, pundits, imams, *shankara-charyas* – millions of priests in the world who depend on a single concept of God. Drop that idea and all these people will be nowhere. Right now they have great prestige, power.

> *"Just as the priest has been afraid that God should not be doubted, the politician has been afraid that the priest should not be doubted."*

God is not there. And with him, the Holy Ghost disappears, the Son disappears. God is the central focus of the whole fiction. Remove that central idea, and the whole palace made of playing cards simply falls on the ground. Just a little whip is needed.

The psychologist is afraid of meditation. Now psychology is a big profession. Jews never do small things. They created this stupid Christianity, and for two thousand years they have been grudging: "We missed the chance. We would have made the great profession, which the Christians are doing. How did we miss Jesus? It was simply a great business, and we missed the point. We couldn't see that this man is going to be such a big deal." He proved the biggest business deal in the world. Jews cannot forgive him. If they get him again they will crucify him again, for another reason this time: "Why didn't you tell us in the first place that this is going to be a big business? – we would not have crucified you."

And then they nearly missed the second – Sigmund Freud – but this time they were more aware, and they have not missed so much. Ninety percent of the profession is still in Jewish hands. All the great psychologists and psychoanalysts and therapists – ninety percent of them are Jews. It is their monopoly. And Freud single-handedly created the whole profession, the whole science. He was very much afraid of meditation, tremendously afraid. Jung, his most intimate disciple, and in the beginning his possible successor, was so afraid of meditation that when he came to India, wherever he went – and he went to Khajuraho, to the Taj Mahal, to Fatehpur Sikri, old, ancient places – everywhere it was suggested to him that, "You should go to Arunachal in the south of India, the very south, deep south. There is a man, Sri Ramana Maharshi, who can give you immense insight into human nature, about which you have been working your whole life," but he was afraid to go there.

And Ramana was certainly the man who could have given him, shared with him, something of meditation. But Jung would not go. Outright he rejected it, saying, "All this meditation is unscientific."

Now, his statement is unscientific, because nobody has tried to explore meditation scientifically. On what grounds is he saying that all this meditation business is unscientific?

I know the space when there is no sleep, no dream, and still I am there. Certainly dreams are needed, but not by me. Perhaps ninety-nine point nine percent of people, or even more, need dreams, six hours of dreams in the night. And do you think that's all? Are you not dreaming in the day too?

Any time, close your eyes and you will find the dream is there, running. The dream is always there. You are listening to me, and a dream will be there. You are walking on the road, and the dream is moving inside you. Of course when you are awake your attention is divided: you have to be alert to the outside world, otherwise people think you are spaced out. You are not spaced out, you are spaced in! Your attention is no longer out. You are clouded with dreams and you have forgotten the objective world. Six hours in the night and how many hours in the day? Nobody has yet measured how many hours in the day. I don't think that you have even two hours in a day, just as you have in the night, without dreams. I don't think you have two hours in a day without dreams, because if you can have two hours without dreams, fully awake, those two hours will become your meditation. They will reveal immensely valuable secrets to you.

But ordinary humanity, the average man, needs dreams. Why? – because life, in reality, is so unsatisfactory, so ugly, so stinkingly ugly. Those dreams substitute for it. They are beautiful. They bring fragrance in your life, hope, fiction. They help you to remain sane. The reality will drive you insane.

And to me, God, the Holy Ghost and the Son, and the pope, the infallible pope… Of course he has to be infallible, he represents the messiah, the only begotten Son of God; how can he be fallible? The "infallible pope"… And every religion has similar things. You need these people – they are fictions created by your misery, and by cunning people using your misery to exploit you and to have their power trip.

> *"Even a mad politician like Adolf Hitler needs the blessings of God. Adolf Hitler is being blessed by God's priest."*

The politician needs these people also. Even a mad politician like Adolf Hitler needs the blessings of God. If there is no God, who is going to bless Adolf Hitler? And the chief Christian priest in Germany blesses him. Now see the miracle: Adolf Hitler is being blessed by God's priest: "You will succeed." Churchill is being blessed in England by the same God's priest: "You will be successful." Benito Mussolini is blessed by the pope himself: "You will be successful." And nobody sees the contradiction: one God, one infallible pope – and this German priest is under the same pope!

But the pope has to bless Benito Mussolini, otherwise Mussolini will throw him out and put in somebody else as the pope who is ready to bless him. Benito Mussolini is not a fascist when he is in power. Even the pope says, "He is the most wise man, the most democratic, most human" – Benito Mussolini! And the same pope, after Benito Mussolini is defeated, will declare him a fascist. And these are infallible people. Now another politician is there who has to be blessed, who is against Benito Mussolini; they will bless him too.

Can't you see a simple conspiracy between the priest and the politician? The masses are befooled. The priest gives the sanction from God, certifies that this is the right man to be the president, this is the right man to be the vice-president, the prime minister. Of course the politician needs it because the masses will listen to the priest: the priest is impartial, he has nothing to do with politics, he is above politics. He is not! The priest is in the hands of the politicians.

The Dalai Lama is the pope, in fact higher than the pope for the Buddhists, because he is not a representative of Jesus, he is a reincarnation of Buddha himself. Not a representative, but a reincarnation of Buddha himself. The Dalai Lama escaped from Tibet because China became Communist and claimed that Tibet is part of China. Once it was – two hundred, three hundred years ago. There was a time when a Chinese emperor conquered Tibet, and Tibet was part of China. And of course the Tibetans and Chinese belong to the same race.

> "Can't you see a simple conspiracy between the priest and the politician?"

The Dalai Lama had to escape from there because he was both the religious head and the political head. And he had never thought that anybody was going to attack Tibet. It is so secluded a country, on top of the world, and so far away from every other place; no railway trains are there, no cars are there, no roads are there: no technology has reached there. People are still living at least five thousand years behind.

He had to escape because he did not have a big army. He had never thought, and his predecessors had never thought, that anybody was going to attack – to attack is so difficult, to reach Tibet is so difficult. But Mao was determined to take it over. It was a very significant place for him not to leave alone because Russia could take it, and then it would become a tremendously dangerous thing for China. India could take it; then too it would become tremendously difficult for China. So before anybody else started thinking, China jumped in. And Tibet is a small country, and the Dalai Lama had just a small police force, perhaps one hundred policemen to guard the palace. That was all, there was no need for anything else. Army? They had never thought about the army.

But the incarnation of Buddha escaped from Tibet, forgot about the people whom he has been exploiting, his predecessors have been exploiting, for thousands of years. Tibet is a poor country, but the Dalai Lama is one of the richest men in the world. The whole palace of Lhasa was filled with gold and nothing else. Strange even to think that the Dalai Lama escaped with all the gold from the Lhasa palace, not all the ancient scriptures – because there was a clear choice: you can take this or you can take... There were so many scriptures that you would need thousands of cars to take them to India. And he had so much gold – and the gold had to reach first, because without gold what was he going to do in India? And the refugees that were following him from Tibet, what were they going to do? So the scriptures were left; gold was carried – this is the incarnation of Buddha!

China immediately crowned his younger brother, Panchen Lama, as the head of the country. The politicians couldn't do without it because the masses won't listen. Now the masses were perfectly happy. What difference does it make – the Dalai Lama or Panchen Lama? He was going to be his successor, he was the second in line. If the Dalai Lama dies, or anything happens, Panchen Lama would become the head. The Dalai Lama has escaped, and China made him a laughingstock: "You believed in him and he deceived you; not only that, he has stolen all your gold."

Now in India, Jawaharlal Nehru was the prime minister when the Dalai Lama came there. He welcomed him. That was his politics, because in India Buddhism was once the religion of almost the whole country. But then after Buddha's death, the Hindus destroyed everything that was possible. So either the Buddhist monks had to escape – that's how Tibet became Buddhist, Ceylon became Buddhist, Japan became Buddhist, China became Buddhist, Korea became Buddhist, Vietnam became Buddhist, Indo-China became Buddhist, Burma became Buddhist, the whole of Asia – except India, where Buddha was born and where he worked and where he transformed people.

In India, Buddhism completely disappeared. Either the Buddhist monk had to leave India or he was killed, burned alive, or reduced to the lowest caste in India – the untouchable, sudra. The *chamars* in India, the shoemakers in India, they are all Buddhists – they were reduced, forced only to make shoes, and do nothing else. In a country like India where vegetarianism is thought to be one of the fundamentals of religion, who is going to kill animals and who is going to make shoes and other leather things? The Buddhists were forced: "If you want to be alive and you want to live here, then choose this profession." Everybody was happy; Hindus and Jainas, all were happy that they had been put in their right place.

But what happened? After independence, one man, Doctor Ambedkar, started converting the *chamars*, the shoemakers, back to Buddhism. He converted thousands of people back to Buddhism. He created a great movement back to Buddhism, and there was a possibility that millions would turn. He died, but still he left a strong force of Buddhism behind

> "The politician has the political power; the priest has the religious power. The politician protects the priest, the priest blesses the politician – and the masses are exploited, sucked; their blood is sucked by both."

him. Now, Nehru wanted this force to be with him. The Dalai Lama was the perfectly right person, because all those Buddhists would listen to the Dalai Lama. And the Dalai Lama had to listen to Jawaharlal, otherwise: "Go back, or go anywhere else you want to go." Jawaharlal gave him space against China. China raised the question: "This will be a surety that we are no longer friends. Hand over the Dalai Lama to us."

They wanted the Dalai Lama in their hands because Panchen Lama is not so powerful. Although the Tibetans have accepted him, the Dalai Lama was their chosen leader. This has been imposed by the Chinese; reluctantly they have accepted. If the Dalai Lama had been given back to China, they would have forced him to be in Tibet, to be the Dalai Lama again, but instructions were received from Mao Zedong: "The country will be under us." Nehru refused to deliver the Dalai Lama to him.

You will be surprised, even a country like America… Just a few years ago the Dalai Lama was invited by American Buddhists, because there are a few Zen monasteries and a few American Buddhists, they had invited the Dalai Lama. The American government stopped him from entering the country because that would create enmity with China. And for America, the Dalai Lama had no meaning because these few Buddhists didn't count.

What I am telling you is that these politicians and these priests have been constantly in conspiracy, working together hand in hand. The politician has the political power; the priest has the religious power. The politician protects the priest, the priest blesses the politician – and the masses are exploited, sucked; their blood is sucked by both.

Remove God and you remove the politicians, you remove the politics, you remove the priest; you remove the conspiracy between the priest and the politician. And with these two removed, fifty percent of your miseries will disappear.

The idea of God gives you dreams of a better life – after death, perhaps in paradise or in another incarnation. So there is not so much to be worried about – this life, it is a small thing, what does it matter? In millions and millions of light years, what does it matter, seventy years? It does not count at all. There are stars so far away from us that the day you were born, their rays started moving on that day toward the earth – they have not reached here yet. You will die, then, perhaps, sometime those rays will reach. And rays move with a tremendous speed, one hundred and eighty-six thousand miles per second. For that star, you never existed. Before you were born and before you died, no ray could reach here to see you, to touch you. As far as that star is concerned…and millions of stars are there, that far away. What to say about you? There are stars whose rays have not reached the earth since the earth came into existence. And it may go out of existence and those stars will never come to know that there has been a planet like earth.

So what to say about your Alexander the Great, Napoleon Bonaparte, Ivan the Terrible? They don't count at all, anywhere, in this vast universe. Seventy years…so religions have been telling people, "Seventy years don't count. This misery will pass away, and if you allow it to pass away without struggling against it, the next life, life beyond death, is going to be very rewarding to you." These are the people who have prevented you from changing any situation on the earth. Particularly, they have prevented the transformation of man, because all the suffering that you see all around is rooted in man. And if man remains the same, this tension will go on increasing, this anguish will go on increasing.

> *"To be a successful politician you have to be absolutely unintelligent, fanatic, lying, promising continuously – knowing perfectly well that no promises are going to be fulfilled – cheating, using beautiful words and hiding ugly realities."*

There is every possibility that by the end of this century the whole of humanity may commit suicide, a global war. And it is not very difficult to imagine its possibility, because the people who are in power, the people who have nuclear weapons, are so third rate. It seems that to be a successful politician you have to be absolutely unintelligent, fanatic, lying, promising continuously – knowing perfectly well that no promises are going to be fulfilled – cheating, using beautiful words and hiding ugly realities.

Now each big, powerful country is loaded with nuclear weapons – so much so that if we want we can destroy seven hundred earths like this right now. That much nuclear power is there, available, to destroy each person seven hundred times – although it is not needed, one time is enough. But politicians don't want to take any chances.

Their faces are all masks: they say one thing, they do another thing. And the power is in such people's hands. Any crackpot can push a button and can finish the whole of humanity, the whole of life on the earth.

But perhaps deep down humanity also wants to get rid of itself. Perhaps individually people are not courageous enough to commit suicide, but on the mass scale they are ready.

Always remember, individuals have not committed great crimes. It is always crowds which commit great crimes, because in a crowd no individual feels, "I am responsible for what is happening." He thinks, "I am just being with the people." Individually when you commit something, you have to think three times before committing it: What are you doing? Is it right? Does your consciousness permit it? But no, when there is a crowd you can be lost in the crowd, nobody will ever discover that you were also part of it.

> *"In a crowd no individual feels, 'I am responsible for what is happening.'"*

Even a country like Germany, which can be said to be one of the most intelligent, cultured, sophisticated countries, has given great poets, painters, scientists, philosophers…in every dimension Germany's contribution is great. But one simply feels amazed that this country of Hegel, Feuerbach, Kant, Marx, Freud, Einstein – this country came under the power of Adolf Hitler, who was nothing but a madman. What happened? Even a man like Martin Heidegger, who was the topmost philosopher of the contemporary world, he supported Adolf Hitler. It is so shocking to think… I have always appreciated the man because his intelligence is incomparable. Other philosophers are miles behind: Sartre, Marcel, Jaspers – miles behind. Nobody is even close to this man; even to understand him is not easy. But he supported Adolf Hitler. And when Germany lost the war and Adolf Hitler committed suicide, then he was as if awakened from a dream. Then he realized what he had done: "This man was simply mad, and I have supported him."

That's what I say: even when your eyes are fully open, you may be dreaming. Now he was dreaming, and he was projecting his dream on Adolf Hitler because he saw that this man has power, has the power to impress the masses, which Martin Heidegger had not. He could not even deliver a single address because everybody would leave. The way he talked, the things he talked about, the complications that he brought in – now who was going to listen to him?

He was a professor of philosophy in the university – in fact in many universities, for the simple reason because wherever he was a professor, students stopped coming to the department. He was far above them. He would go above your head; and if this man was going to be your examiner too, you were finished. And when he had been there for two, three years in one university, then the university would say to him, "Move; nobody is going to come here." Then finally they decided to make him the vice-chancellor of the university so he did not teach.

He had no power over the masses, and he saw Adolf Hitler – the masses were just spellbound, almost in a state of hypnosis. So he projected what he dreamed – how the world should be – this man could make it possible.

But he was innocent. He did not understand that this man had his own mad ideas what he was going to do to the world. He was not going to listen to any philosopher. And Martin Heidegger at least was absolutely beyond him. Hitler would not even have made intelligible conversation with him.

The religions have given man fictions to live. Now all those fictions are broken and man has nothing left to live for – hence the anguish. Anguish is not an ordinary state of anxiety. Anxiety is always centered upon a certain problem. You don't have money, there is anxiety; you don't have enough clothes and the cold is coming, you have a certain anxiety; you are sick and you don't have medicine, and there is anxiety. Anxiety is about a certain problem. Anguish has no problem as such. Just to *be* seems to be fruitless, futile. Just to breathe seems to be dragging yourself unnecessarily, because what is going to happen tomorrow? Yesterday also you were thinking that something is going to happen tomorrow. Now, this is yesterday's tomorrow, which has come as today, and nothing has happened. And this has been going on for years, and you go on projecting for tomorrow. A moment comes when you start realizing that nothing is going to happen. Then there is the state of anguish.

In anguish, only one thing seems to be there: somehow to get out of this circle of life – hence suicide, the increasing rate of suicide. And an unconscious desire of humanity that the third world war happens: "So I am not responsible that I committed suicide. The world war killed everybody, and killed me too."

But the whole situation can be changed. We just have to change the premises of the old man: remove God, remove heaven and hell, remove the idea of a future reward – remove the idea that some messiah is going to come to redeem you from your suffering. Remove the idea that anybody else is responsible for your misery and suffering; remove the idea that somebody else can give meaning to your life. Accept that you are alone – born alone, and you will die alone. And you have to accept the fact that you are living alone – maybe in a crowd, but you are living alone; maybe with your wife, girlfriend, boyfriend, but they are alone in their aloneness, you are alone in your aloneness, and those alonenesses don't touch each other, never touch each other.

You may live with someone for twenty years, thirty years, fifty years – it makes no difference, you will remain strangers. Always and always you will be strangers. Accept the fact: "We are strangers. I don't know who you are, you don't know who I am. I myself don't know who I am, so how can you know?" But people are presuming that the husband should know the wife, the husband is assuming the wife should know the husband. Everybody is functioning as if everybody is a mind reader and he should know your needs, your problems, before you say it. He should know, she should know – and they should do something.

> "You may live with someone for twenty years, thirty years, fifty years – it makes no difference, you will remain strangers."

Now this is all nonsense! Nobody knows you, not even you, so don't expect that anybody else should know you; it is not possible in the very nature of things. We are strangers. Perhaps by chance we have met and we are together, but our aloneness is there. Don't forget it, because you have to work upon it. Only from there is your redemption, your salvation.

But you are doing just the opposite: how to forget your aloneness? The boyfriend, the girlfriend, go to the movie, the football match, get lost in the crowd, dance in the disco, forget yourself, drink alcohol, take drugs – but somehow don't let this aloneness come to your conscious mind.

And there lies the whole secret. You have to accept your aloneness, which in no way can you avoid. And there is no way to change its nature. It is your authentic reality. It is you. And you are escaping from yourself. Then there will be misery, there will be problems. And in solving one problem you will create ten more, and so on and so forth. Soon there will be only problems surrounding you, and you will be drowning in your own problems. Then you call out, "Why are the tensions increasing? Why is there so much suffering? Why is there so much misery?" As if somebody has a readymade answer for it.

Yes, somebody has it; it is *you*.

Because I have found the answer within me, hence I say it to you with authority. The authority is not derived from any God, from any messiah, from any Veda, from any Koran, Bible, no. The authority is derived from my experience. My whole life I have lived among millions of people, but never for a single moment forgetting that I am alone – that my aloneness is unreachable; nobody can reach it. It is available only to me, because it *is* me.

So the moment you stop escaping from yourself, drowning yourself in all kinds of drugs, relationships, religions, service to humanity… Now a few are doing that; it is nothing but escape from themselves. But their ego is fulfilled because they are doing service to humanity. I know many "servants," great servants of humanity. And when I talked with them and brought them to the point, nailed them down exactly, they all broke into tears and said, "Perhaps you are right — we are escaping. We were thinking we were going to serve these poor people, but it seems that we have not been able even to solve any of our own problems. This seemed to be a preferable escape; you can put aside your problems. And how can you be so selfish, to be bothered by your problems when the whole of humanity is suffering? When everybody is suffering, help them."

So you can, in a beautiful garb, put aside your problems, decide that even to think about them is selfish. But with those problems, who are you going to help and how? You will dump all your problems on somebody who you are going to serve. The husband will dump on the wife, the wife will dump on the husband. The parents will dump on the children, and everybody is dumping his problems on others without seeing that the other is also trying to do the same.

Stop dumping problems on others. You have to solve your problems, and every individual has to solve his own problems. And the problems are not so many. It is one problem, which you have not solved, that has created a chain of unsolved problems.

The problem is: how to enter your aloneness without fear? And the moment you enter your aloneness without fear, it is such a beautiful and ecstatic experience that there is nothing compared to it. It is not a problem at all. It is the solution of all your problems. But you have made it a problem because you have listened to others and followed them: the blind following blind leaders and priests, and they are all going in a circle, and everybody believes that the man ahead of him is capable of seeing, and the same is the case with the man who is ahead. He is holding somebody else's coat or shirt, believing that he knows where he is going, and they all are moving in a circle; nobody is going anywhere. The followers are following the leader, the leader is following the followers....

> "You have to stop and come out of this stupid game of followers and leaders."

You have to stop and come out of this stupid game of followers and leaders. You have just to be yourself and remember that you were born alone, so aloneness is your reality. That you will die alone, so aloneness is your reality. And between birth and death, between these two points where you are absolutely alone, how can life be anything else? It is, in each moment, alone. So accept it joyously; go into it as much as possible, as many times as possible.

This is the temple of my religion. It is not made of rocks, marble. It is made of your consciousness. Go into it. And the deeper you go, the farther away are the problems. The moment you touch the center of your being, you have arrived home.

And from that point, you can come out and do whatsoever you want to do. It will be a help, it will be service. It will be sharing. You will not be dumping anything on anybody.

On the one hand, the priest has given you the desire for the other world, the ambition for the other world, for a tomorrow.

The politician is giving you this world: you can become the president, anybody in America can become the president, all citizens are equal.

What nonsense! No two citizens are equal. And only the most cunning is going to become the president, not all. At least not those who would have been of any help to anybody. Only ambitious people can reach the highest political post in any country because it is a race, and you need to be utterly ambitious to stake everything on it. And you are not to bother what you are doing, whether it is right or wrong. You have to keep the end in mind and do whatsoever you feel right to reach the end; whether it is right or wrong, no question. If you fail, everything is wrong; if you succeed, everything is right. Success is right and failure is wrong. That's the way politicians have been training everybody.

Drop all that the priests and the politicians have put into you. And as you unburden yourself, you start having glimpses of your pure being. That's what I call meditation. Once tasted, it transforms forever.

CHAPTER 3

Poverty, Chastity, and Obedience

All that is needed is to uproot the conditionings that the priests have put into you. The priests put those conditionings into you so that they could become mediators and agents between you and God, so that your direct contact was cut. Naturally you would need somebody else to connect you, and the priest would become powerful. And the priest *has* been powerful down the ages. Whosoever can put you in contact with power, real power, will become powerful.

God is real power, the source of all power. The priest remained so powerful down the ages – more powerful than kings. Now the scientist has taken the place of the priest, because now he knows how to unlock the doors of the power hidden in nature. The priest knew how to connect you with God, the scientist knows how to connect you with nature. But the priest has to disconnect you first, so no individual private line remains between you and God. He has spoiled your inner sources, poisoned them. He became very powerful, but the whole humanity became lustless, loveless, full of guilt.

My people have to drop that guilt completely. While making love, think of prayerful, meditation, godliness. While making love, burn incense, chant, sing, dance. Your bedroom should be a temple, a sacred place. And lovemaking should not be a hurried thing. Go deeper into it; savor it as slowly, as gracefully as possible. And you will be surprised. You have the key.

Existence has not sent you into the world without keys. But those keys have to be used, you have to put them into the lock and turn them.

Love is another phenomenon, one of the most potential, where the ego disappears and you are conscious, fully conscious, pulsating, vibrating. You are no longer an individual, you are lost into the energy of the whole.

Then, slowly, slowly let this become your very way of life. What happens at the peak of love has to become your discipline – not just an experience but a discipline. Then whatever you are doing and wherever you are walking…early in the morning with the sun rising, have the same feeling, the same merger with existence. Lying down on the ground, the sky full of stars, have the same merger again. Lying down on the earth, feel one with the earth.

Slowly, slowly lovemaking should give you the clue how to be in love with existence itself. And then the ego is known as a fiction, is used as a fiction. And using it as a fiction, there is no danger.

There are a few other moments when the ego slips of its own accord. In moments of great danger: you are driving and suddenly you see an accident is going to happen. You have lost control of the car and there seems to be no possibility of saving yourself. You are going to crash into the tree or into the oncoming truck, or you are going to fall into the river, it is so absolutely certain. In those moments suddenly the ego will disappear.

That's why there is a great attraction to move into dangerous situations. People climb Everest. It is a deep meditation; they may or may not understand this. Mountaineering is of great importance. Climbing mountains is dangerous – the more dangerous it is, the more beautiful. You will have glimpses, great glimpses of egolessness. Whenever danger is very close, the mind stops. The mind can think only when you are not in danger; it has nothing to say in danger. Danger makes you spontaneous and in that spontaneity, you suddenly know that you are not the ego.

Or – this will be for different people, because people are

different – if you have an aesthetic heart, then beauty will open the doors. Just seeing a beautiful woman or a man passing by, just for a single moment a flash of beauty, and suddenly the ego disappears. You are overwhelmed. Or seeing a lotus in the pond, or seeing the sunset or a bird on the wing – anything that triggers your inner sensitivity, anything that possesses you for the moment so deeply that you forget yourself, that you are and yet you are not, that you abandon yourself – then too the ego slips. It is a fiction; you have to carry it. If you forget it for a moment, it slips.

And it is good that there are a few moments when it slips and you have a glimpse of the true and the real. It is because of these glimpses that religion has not died. It is not because of the priests – they have done everything to kill it. It is not because of the so-called religious, those who go to the church and the mosque and the temple. They are not religious at all, they are pretenders.

Religion has not died, because of these few moments which happen more or less to almost everybody. Take more note of them, imbibe the spirit of those moments more, allow those moments more, create spaces for those moments to happen more. This is the true way to seek God. Not to be in the ego is to be godly.

Just a few days ago, someone wrote me a letter saying, "Osho, You have created a trouble" – because I had said some time ago that many people, almost the majority of people in the world, men and women both, are untrained lovers. No training has been given to them. In fact everything has been kept from them, they have been kept ignorant. What does a virgin mean? Someone who has been kept absolutely ignorant. So I had said that the best way to introduce your children to love will be that while you are making love, children should be playing around. Let them be there. And in fact it is one of the most significant things, because every child sooner or later discovers what you are doing to his mother. First he thinks that this father seems to be a barbarian, doing pushups on the poor woman. He wants to kill this man, but the child is so small…so he represses the desire, and he is not even allowed to admit that he has seen it.

And the child will never be able to forgive you, that you were secretive about things. You were not open, even with him. You talked about love, but love means many things: openness, honesty, sincerity. And about one of the most basic things in life, you kept the child absolutely unaware.

> "Those who go to the church and the mosque and the temple. They are not religious at all, they are pretenders."

Children are very intelligent. Every child is born with a tremendous energy of intelligence. It is the society and the education and the religion – they start destroying his intelligence, so by the time he is a young man he is just a fool. But small children are very perceptive, you cannot deceive them. So I had said that it is perfectly good – because the child has to learn and it is better he learns from the very beginning.

Now this woman wrote to me, "A problem has arisen: we allowed our child to be present while we were making love; now the child wants to make love to me. He says, 'If father can do it, why can't I do it?' Now we cannot say that this is sin, because if it is sin, then why is his father doing it, and why is he being allowed to commit sin?"

In a really human society there will be no sexual abuse of children. Such abuse exists only because children are kept in the dark; and they are curious, very curious, "What is it all about?" Then they get caught in somebody's net.

But children are very understanding too. The mother, the father, both should make him understand, "This is your training to see how love is made. The time will come when you will be a young man and you will be making love – then don't make the same mistakes that we have made."

Make your lovemaking a deep understanding for the child. Make him also aware that he is not your age. Make the place of your lovemaking a temple, so that the child from the very beginning starts feeling love is something sacred. And if he knows everything about it, nobody can abuse him.

Now the question arises: who is responsible for sexual abuse of the child? You are responsible. You are keeping your children in darkness, and they are feeling that there is something that is being kept secret. They become curious; the more you hide it, the more curious they are.

If it is open and is made available so the child can understand it – yes, there will be a few problems, like the child wanting to make love to the mother. The mother can hug the child, the mother can help the child to understand: "Just look at my size and your size. Just grow up and you will find a beautiful woman, far more beautiful than me."

But every mother wants the child to feel that she is the greatest and the most beautiful woman in the world, not knowing that she is creating a tragedy for the child for his whole life because now he will be looking for her all around the world and he will not find her. No woman will come up to the standard of his mother. No woman is going to give him satisfaction.

The same is true about small girls. They should be made absolutely aware – not just verbally in a classroom. That does not help, they become even more curious.

Make it very honest. And when the experiment is happening every day in the house, where is the problem? Let your girl, your boy, be present. Let them see the beauty of it. Make the whole phenomenon as sacred as possible. And these children will always respect you because you were so honest with them, so sincere with them; you never kept anything secret from them.

And any problems like this – boys asking to make love to their mother – can be explained to them, that they are not yet ripe. One day they will be ripe; for that day we are preparing them. And children are very receptive, very understanding.

There is sexual abuse of children because they are kept in darkness by their parents, by their teachers. Love is something like a sin which has to be done in darkness, and nobody is to know about it. You are doing something ugly – in your own mind it is something ugly, something that should not be done. You are not rejoicing in it.

Rejoice! Make love a festive moment. And of course, your children have to take part in it. They can at least dance around you while you are making love, sing beautiful songs around you, play on their small guitars, drums. They can make it really festive! And they will understand that they are children and they are not of age, and soon they will get their own lovers. And if this experience has been part of their growing up, their love life will have a totally different flavor.

So in child abuse, the person who has abused the child is only a victim of a very neurotic society. From the very childhood every child has to be made aware of all possibilities of love, sex, and all deviations, perversions. Then there will be no sexual abuse of children.

The man of awareness is not in search of judgments, condemnation, appraisal. He is simply witnessing, with clarity. His clarity tells him what is right, without any effort – your effort is not needed. It is the easiest thing for the man of awareness to know what is right and what is wrong. And also he will be able to see why something wrong goes on happening. There must be roots somewhere in the culture, in the society, in the world, that poisonous flowers go on flowering. And somebody must be taking care of those plants, watering them. Your priests are doing it, your politicians are doing it, your psychoanalysts are doing it, your professors are doing it – because these people live on your misery. They live on your being somewhere wrong. If you are perfectly right, they are useless.

Goethe once wrote in his Goetz von Berlichingen, "Poverty, chastity and obedience – unbearable are they all." What do you think about his statement?

It is absolutely correct. These are the three calamities that have ruined the very being of humanity.

Obedience means, in other words, slavery. We are very clever to use good words for ugly realities. I do not teach you *disobedience*;

this has to be understood clearly. Obedience is ugly, and the human mind moves like a pendulum of a clock – it immediately goes to the opposite. Then it starts making disobedience the law of life. Disobedience is only a reaction. If there is no obedience imposed on you, disobedience will disappear automatically because there is nothing to disobey. So I have to make it clear to you that I hate obedience, but in that obedience, disobedience is included because they are part of one reality.

I teach intelligence.

Obedience keeps you retarded. You have just to follow; you are not to doubt, you are not to question, you have just to be a robot. Naturally, sooner or later, particularly younger people start feeling that all this obedience is nothing but a strategy to impose slavery. They react and move to the other extreme. Whatever is said, don't do it – that becomes their religion. In both ways they remain retarded.

> "The man of awareness is not in search of judgments, condemnation, appraisal."

My struggle is against the retardedness of human mind. I want you to be intelligent, to decide for yourself.

I can explain something to you. I can put all my cards open before you. Now it is up to you to decide what to do. Action is going to be your decision.

Explanation can be done by your parents, by your teachers, by the society, but explanation is not an order to act. They are simply making you aware of the whole situation. Making you aware of the whole situation makes you intelligent; you become more alert, you start seeing things which you were not seeing before. You become aware of new directions, new dimensions, new ways of looking at things. But there is no order that you have to act according to the explanation given to you.

Action has to come from your own intelligence, from your own understanding. It will not be obedience, it will not be disobedience. Sometimes you may feel it perfectly right to do something, but that is your decision. Sometimes you may feel it is not right to do something; that too is your decision. The more decisions you are allowed to take, the more your intelligence is sharpened.

Obedience takes away the very base of growth. It simply orders you. You can see it happening in the army: the very psychology of obedience in its complete picture. The soldiers are for years trained for absolutely meaningless things. "Turn to the left"...there is no reason. "Turn to the right"...there is no reason. Go backward, come forward, there is no reason. For hours! It is an exercise in destroying intelligence.

I have heard of a professor in the Second World War. When everybody was needed for the army, he was also recruited. And he was stating continuously, "You don't understand. I am a professor of philosophy. I will not be able to become a soldier because I cannot even take a single step without deciding why." But nobody listened to him, and the first day on the parade ground when the commander ordered "Turn to the left," everybody turned except the professor.

The commander was informed beforehand, "He is a little eccentric; he is a professor of philosophy, so be patient with him." He didn't say anything. Then the people were ordered to turn to the right, go backward, come forward, but the professor remained in his position. When everybody had come back to the same position, the commander asked the professor, "Why were you not following the orders?"

He said, "It is so stupid...because if finally everybody has to come to this stage where I am already standing, then what was all that, 'Come back, go forward, go right, go left'? If this was going to be the final order, then I am already there. What more do you want? And I want to ask, why have these people been treated like machines?"

It was impossible to answer! There is no why; it is a strategy to destroy intelligence. When a person just follows orders for years, morning and evening, he forgets completely that he has his own decisiveness. The order becomes his decision.

The commander reported to the higher authorities, "That man is impossible, he argues."

In the army no argument is allowed. They said, "Give him some small job in the mess, where there is no question of ordering."

So he was brought into the mess, given a pile of peas, and he was told, "Within one hour you have to sort out the bigger peas on one side and the smaller peas on the other side." He listened. After one hour, when the commander came, he was sitting silently and the pile was also sitting silently exactly as it was left. The commander said, "Now what is the problem?"

He said, "The problem is this: unless I figure out everything beforehand in detail, I never move. There are peas which are big, there are peas which are small, but there are peas which are in the middle. Where am I put to the peas which are in the middle? Rather than doing something wrong, it is better not to do anything. And this hour was beautiful. I meditated, the peas meditated, and everything was silent. No left turn, right turn... I love this job." And he had not done anything.

The whole structure of armies around the world is made in such a way that in three or four years they destroy your intelligence completely, you become almost a mechanical robot. The moment you hear the order, "March!" you simply march; no question arises within you.

After the First World War, a man was retired. He had been awarded great prizes for his bravery. Two people sitting in a restaurant watched the man carrying a bucket full of eggs on his head, and just to play a joke, one of them shouted, "Attention!"

In the middle of the street, the man stood in the position of attention and the eggs fell all over the street. He was very angry. He said, "This is not right. Now who is going to pay for my eggs?"

Those people said, "We have done nothing. There is no prohibition on using the word *attention*. We have not told you to obey it."

The man said, "You don't understand. I have been thirty years in the army. I have completely forgotten how to make any decision on my own – attention means simply attention. Although I am retired, the habit of thirty years of simply being obedient has become my second nature. I am a poor man. You should not have done this."

Obedience is basically used by religions, politicians, educationalists, parents. They are all destroying your intelligence, and they are making a great value of obedience. It is a disease far more dangerous than any cancer, because cancer can be cured, can be operated on.

But once you get caught in the net of obedience, there is no cure for you.

God was angry with Eve and Adam because they disobeyed; that was their only sin. Obedience is virtue. And the disobedience of Adam and Eve was so great that even now every Christian is born in sin, because your original forefathers – Adam and Eve – sinned against God. Obedience seems to be the very base of all your religions. In different ways they support it: belief, faith, no questioning, simply following the Holy Bible or the holy Koran. You are not taken into account at all. You are just a slave.

Certainly obedience makes you more efficient. That's why everybody wants you to be obedient – your father, your mother, everybody wants you to be obedient.

> "Obedience is basically used by religions, politicians, educationalists, parents. They are all destroying your intelligence."

In my childhood it was an everyday problem. I had made it clear to my parents, "If you want me to do something, please explain to me why, and let me decide. If you don't want me to do it, then you can order me to do it. I would rather die than follow your order."

In my village we had a beautiful river. In summer it was not so big, but in the rainy season it became huge. I was a constant lover of the river, and if they could not find me anywhere else they searched for me near the river, and they always found me there.

My father told me, "Remember one thing: when the river is flooded with rainwater, it is a mountainous river, do not try to cross it."

I said, "Now it is absolutely impossible for me to resist the temptation. I will cross it."

He said, "You will die. You will not be able to cross such a strong, mountainous current."

I said, "It will be a glorious death, but I am going to cross it."

The whole village gathered when I crossed the river. I was only twelve years of age. Nobody had done it before, it looked so dangerous. It took me almost six miles downstream to reach the other shore, and many times I felt that it was going to be impossible. But I crossed it. Later on my father said to me, "Can't you understand anything?"

I said, "That's what I am trying to do, but you don't let me understand."

I had made it clear to the whole family, "Don't order; otherwise I am not going to obey. You are making me disobedient. The whole crime will be on your heads. I simply want to have explanations and to be left at liberty to decide for myself. You should have explained to me the whole situation of the river, how dangerous it can be, and that is all; then it would have been my decision to do it or not to do it. But it has to be my decision, not anybody else's. I understand your intention is good, but the way you are trying to impose your intention is very dangerous. Rather than seeing the death of my intelligence I would like to die myself, because what is the point of living like a robot?"

So Goethe is correct: obedience is one of the greatest sins. All the religions have perpetuated it, and all the generations have perpetuated it.

He is absolutely right when he says about chastity that it is unbearable. It is not only unbearable – he is not being absolutely correct – it is impossible. Chastity is against nature, and in anything against nature you are going to be a loser. You can be victorious *with* nature – against it, your defeat is sure and certain. But that's what for centuries we have been told, to be chaste – and at a time when it is naturally and absolutely impossible. At the age of fourteen the boy becomes sexually mature; nature is ready, the boy is capable of reproducing. At thirteen the girl is ready to reproduce. But all the societies prolong things: there is education, the university…

The scientific fact is that between fourteen and twenty-one, somewhere near eighteen and a half, the boy comes to the very highest peak of sexual energy, which he will never attain again. And the same is true with the girl: somewhere near seventeen and a half she comes to the greatest peak of attaining orgasmic experience.

The whole of humanity has been deprived of orgasmic experience. By the time somebody returns from the university he is twenty-five, and if he goes back there for a PhD then he is twenty-seven or twenty-eight. His peak of sexual energy is gone – down the drain! And now he gets married. Both are declining, and now they are no longer capable of having that vigor, that natural force which could have produced the orgasmic experience – which is one of the foundations of religious experience.

A person who has known orgasmic blissfulness, only for a few moments, has touched the boundary line that divides ordinary life from the divine life. And with the orgasmic experience the desire naturally arises, "Is it all, or is there much more?" The experience is so tremendously thrilling that one wants to have something more, something better, something more refined. The first person who became religious must have become religious only because of orgasmic experience – because there is no other experience which can give you an insight into religion.

Millions of people on the earth live their whole lives without the orgasmic experience. You want these people to pray in churches, in the temples, in mosques? You have destroyed the very energy in them which would have taken them to the beyond without any priest.

In the orgasmic experience a few things become very clear to the person: one, mind stops – for a few seconds there are no thoughts. Time stops – for a few moments there is no past, no future, but only the present. Of course the experience is very fleeting and very momentary. And the only drawback in it is that it depends on the other person; it happens between two persons – a man and a woman who are deep in love, who want to merge into each other so totally that they are not two entities but one organic whole.

It is a very simple, intelligent understanding that if we can stop thinking and stop time, perhaps the same experience will happen without the other partner. And that's how the whole spiritual phenomenon developed. People tried; they succeeded.

Mind stops and time stops – simultaneously. Mind and time are not two different things. Reality is only in the present; the past and the future are part of the mind. The present is the stoppage of time. When there are no thoughts, how can you think of the past and how can you think of the future? There is no way to think about the present, you are already in it. There is no need to think about it, you are experiencing it.

People tried, explorers of the interior world – we don't know their names, who were the first explorers of the greatest discovery in human existence, who tried and succeeded in stopping time and mind. And they were surprised that when there is not the other, then this state of orgasmic blissfulness can last as long as you want. It is no longer physiology; it is no longer biology; it is no longer genetics – you have come beyond. It can spread over all your twenty-four hours. Slowly, slowly you will start living in it. You don't have to produce it; it becomes just like breathing – you don't even have to think about it.

This state of your consciousness is the greatest experience that life makes available to you. But before it becomes available you should have some taste, some experience that helps you to go in search for the ultimate. This is the ultimate state.

Enlightenment is nothing but an orgasmic state which has become natural to you, just like the heartbeat.

And then there are many discoveries which happen in this state. In this state it was discovered that each man is both a man and a woman, and each woman is both a man and a woman. In the contemporary world, Carl Gustav Jung was the first to come across it. He thought he had discovered something great – it is something great, but it is not his discovery. In the East for at least ten thousand years we have known the fact: there are scriptures…there were statues made in which one half is male and the other half is female.

> "Enlightenment is nothing but an orgasmic state which has become natural to you, just like the heartbeat."

When you are in an orgasmic state, you discover for the first time that no outside woman is needed, no outside man is needed; your own inner woman is meeting with your inner man. And because both are inside you, the meeting can last forever.

Only this kind of person transcends sex. Repression is not

chastity; repression is not celibacy. Repression is perversion. Using sex at the right moment, when it is at its peak...

We are prohibiting our children from having anything to do with sex at the time when they are at the highest peak to which they will never attain again. Now it will be completely going down and down the hill. And when your energies are shrinking, orgasmic experience becomes more and more difficult, almost impossible. Goethe is absolutely right.

Poverty is the third thing he says is unbearable. It is unbearable, but religions have made it bearable. They function as opium – opium can make anything bearable. I have seen this happen in India. Poor women have to go to work; only the husband's earnings are not enough to keep them alive. But they have children, small children, and nobody wants a woman bringing the child to work. If a road is being made, the woman will have to go a dozen times to the child to feed him, to take care of him, and the child will throw tantrums and will cry and weep, and the woman will have to go to calm him down. This is a disturbance.

So they have found a trick. All these poor women give a little opium to the child when they go to work. Then, hungry, in the hot sun, he does not make any trouble; he simply lies down by the side of the road. I have seen hundreds of children lying by the side of the road and the women are working. I was puzzled in the beginning: why are these children so patient? Then I was made aware that they had been given opium.

All the religions have been doing the same to make poverty bearable. The opium is very subtle. First, they all teach that whatever state you are in – in the East it is because of your past life – if you don't make any trouble, if you don't make any revolt against your present state, in the future life you will enjoy all the riches possible. Now, this is psychological opium. Those people are waiting for a future life to have all the pleasures, and somehow carrying their poverty – which is unbearable.

In the West, where past life and future life are not part of the mythologies, they have other consolations. Jesus says, "Blessed are the poor for they shall inherit the kingdom of God." What is this? –

simple opium, to call the poor "blessed." And to console them he says, "A camel can pass through the eye of a needle, but a rich man cannot enter paradise." So the poor man is in a better condition than the rich man. It is only a question of a few years – because there is only one life in Christianity, in Judaism, in Mohammedanism. This is a test of your trust: if you trust in God, if you trust in Jesus Christ, you will go through this very easily. And the whole paradise for eternity is specially made for you; all rich men will be thrown into hell.

> *"'Blessed are the poor for they shall inherit the kingdom of God.' What is this? – simple opium, to call the poor 'blessed.'"*

It gives great consolation. One starts thinking, "That's perfect. We may be poor for seventy years, but these rich people are going to suffer for eternity and we are going to enjoy all the pleasures for eternity. It is not a bad bargain."

If these religions were not giving people such poisonous ideas, the world would have destroyed poverty long, long ago. Man is capable of reaching the moon, and he cannot destroy poverty. He is capable of creating nuclear weapons which can destroy the earth seven hundred times, and he's not capable of destroying poverty. It's simply illogical, absurd.

Poverty can be destroyed, but nobody wants to destroy it. Religions want to keep it, because otherwise all the blessed people of the earth will disappear and there will only be cursed people enjoying. That will be unbearable for the bishops and the cardinals and the pope – the cursed people are enjoying everything and all the blessed people have disappeared. And these blessed people who have disappeared – these blessed people are the people who go to the church; these blessed people are the people who support all kinds of idiots who pretend to be mediators between them and God.

All these religions are living on poverty. The poor go to the churches because they are suffering; it is unbearable, they need some kind of consolation. The rich don't go there; they are not suffering. And if they are in a certain anguish, these priests are not capable of helping them. The rich people, feeling frustrated, have to search for somebody who can help them out of their anguish. They don't want opium.

The politicians don't want everybody to become rich because it is more difficult to enslave rich people than poor. It is easier to purchase the votes of the poor than to convince the rich people to vote for them. The richer a person becomes, the more out of hand he is as far as politicians are concerned. A richer person, if he has any psychological problem, will go to a psychoanalyst, not to a priest. He will go the East to find some meditator to help him realize himself so that he can go beyond the mind, but he will not go to these ordinary priests who don't know anything.

Goethe is right, but nobody has criticized him for the simple reason that he does not elaborate. He simply says, "Chastity, obedience, poverty are unbearable" – in a very mild tone, so nobody has criticized him. He is criticizing your whole church, your whole religion, your whole civilization. But he is being clever, he is not straightforward; he should have defined everything that he meant by it.

I have been told by many sympathetic people – Indira Gandhi was prime minister of India; she told me, "If you say the same things without making them too elaborate and in a mild tone, nobody will make any objection. But you make everything so fiery…"

> "The politicians don't want everybody to become rich because it is more difficult to enslave rich people than poor."

I said, "Then what will be the point? Why should I waste my time making mild, liberal statements if it does not create thinking in people? I am going to put more and more fire into my words."

She said, "I know you. Because of your words I want to come to see you at your commune. I cannot come; I am afraid of my voters, that there will be great trouble. Just coming to meet you in your commune I will lose many voters, many sympathizers." This is from a very courageous woman. And from many sources people have been telling me, "Why don't you say things in such a way that nobody is hurt?"

The point is not that nobody is hurt; if nobody is hurt then nobody wakes up. I am ready to risk my life if I can wake people.

Those three words he has chosen are perfectly right. Goethe was a man of insight, tremendous insight, but not courageous, so that great statement has never been taken any note of by the people – nobody has bothered about it. But now that I have explained what he really means, you can understand that there are many people in the world who have said right things, but in such a lousy way that they don't make any impact.

Humanity needs people who are real fire and who can make them aflame. Certainly many enemies will be created, but that does not count. What counts is the friends. Do you know how many enemies Gautam Buddha created? You cannot name even a few of them. They disappeared, but his friends took over the whole of Asia. How many enemies did Jesus create? – almost the whole of the Jewish community. But where are the enemies? What is their position? What is their situation? Christianity has become the greatest religion in the world, and Jesus had very few friends. To begin with, he had only twelve disciples, a few sympathizers. I am far more fortunate. I have millions of friends. I don't care about the enemies because enemies disappear; they don't make any impact on history.

The impact that is made is made by friends. The friends of truth are the people who revolutionize, who change human beings for the better.

CHAPTER 4

Blessed Are the Poor

The people like Mother Teresa, who have been helping the poor for centuries, are really the causes for poverty continuing. The poor cannot be helped the way Mother Teresa is helping. This is not help, this is politics, because all those orphans she helps are transformed, converted, into Catholic Christianity.

In fact, Mother Teresa would be out of a job if there were no orphans in India. She needs more orphans. That's why they are all against birth control methods, against abortion. Otherwise, from where are you going to get orphans? They need the poor, because without the poor whom are you going to serve? And without service you cannot reach heaven. This is a simple strategy to reach heaven.

I love one story: It happened in China that a man fell into a well. It was the annual fair, so there was so much noise that nobody took any note that he was shouting, "Save me!"

A Buddhist monk passed by; he looked into the well and told the man that there was no need to cry and scream: "Accept whatsoever is the case, be contented. In the next life you will be fulfilled a thousandfold."

The man in the well said, "I am not here to listen to philosophy. I am dying and you are talking philosophy? First, please help me get out."

The Buddhist said, "It is against my religion to interfere in the actions and the consequences of somebody else. You must have committed some sin in your past life. You have fallen into the well – be happy that your sin is finished, your punishment is over. But I am not going to take you out because if tomorrow you murder somebody, then I will also be responsible for it. I am not going to be responsible for any murder." And he went away.

The man could not believe it, "These Buddhists talk about compassion. I am dying and he talks philosophy. I am not in a state even to understand what he is saying."

And after him came a Confucian monk. In the old days in China the wells had no walls surrounding them, so it was very easy to fall into them in the darkness; there was no preventive measure. The Confucian monk said, "Listen, you are the proof of what my master has said. My master has said that every well should have walls around it. Don't be worried, I am going to create a great revolution in the whole country, so that every well is well-protected."

The man said, "But when will the revolution happen? And when will all the wells have walls? By that time I will be gone!"

The Confucian said, "You are not the question – individuals come and go. It is a question for the whole society. We cannot bother about a single individual, we think in terms of the whole civilization." And he went away to create a revolution.

And then came a Christian monk with a bag hanging on his shoulder. He took a rope from the bag, threw it in, took the man out. The man was immensely grateful, fell at his feet and said, "You are the only religious man. But tell me how you guessed that somebody has fallen into the well. And you came with a rope – why are you carrying a rope?"

He said, "We carry everything in this bag for emergency purposes, anywhere. Somebody will need to be served, and our lord Jesus Christ has said that those who serve will receive immense rewards in heaven."

Now, think of a world where nobody is in need of anybody's service: everybody is happy, healthy, comfortable, luxurious. What will happen to the great Christian servants and saints? They will simply be out of a job. They need poverty to remain; it is their very source of becoming saints, holier than thou.

I don't say to my people, "Go and serve the poor." Service, to me, is not a beautiful word. I say to my people, "If you have something, share it. But remember one thing: there is no reward beyond it." Enjoy sharing – that is the reward. If you pull somebody out who is drowning in a well, that's a great joy. What more reward do you want? You saved a life; you should be immensely happy. The reward is in the act itself, and the punishment also is in the act itself. They are not extrinsic, they are intrinsic.

But all these religions have been telling people that the reward is somewhere far away – beyond death – and punishment, too. Neither can it be proved or disproved; hence their business goes on and on, and mediocre people go on following it.

What can I do about a beggar? Whether I give him a rupee or not, he will remain a beggar all the same.

The beggar is not the problem. If the beggar was the problem then everybody who passes by would feel the same; if the beggar was the problem then beggars would have disappeared long ago. The problem is within you: your heart feels it.

Try to understand it. The mind interferes immediately whenever the heart feels love. The mind immediately interferes, the mind says, "Whether you give him something or not, he will remain a beggar all the same."

Whether he remains a beggar or not is not your responsibility – but if your heart feels to do something, do it. Don't try to avoid. The mind is trying to avoid the situation. The mind says, "What is going to happen? He will remain a beggar, so there is no need to do anything." You have missed an opportunity where your love could have flowed. If the beggar has decided to be a beggar, you cannot do anything. You may give him money, he may throw it away. That is for him to decide.

The mind is very clever.

Then the question goes on; it says, "Why are there beggars at all?"

Because there is no love in the human heart. But again, the mind interferes: "Haven't the rich taken away from the poor? Shouldn't the poor take back what the rich have stolen from him?"

Now you are forgetting the beggar and the heartache you felt. Now the whole thing is becoming political, economic. Now the problem is no longer of the heart, it is of the mind. And the mind has created the beggar! It is the cunningness, the calculativeness of the mind that has created the beggar. There are cunning people, very calculative: they have become rich. There are innocent people, not so calculative, not so cunning: they have become poor.

You can change the society – in Soviet Russia they changed the society. That makes no difference. The old categories disappeared, the poor and the rich, but a new category, the ruler and the ruled came up. Now the cunning are the rulers and the innocent are the ruled. Before, the innocent used to be poor and the cunning used to be rich. What can you do? Unless the division between mind and heart is dissolved, unless humanity starts living through the heart and not through the mind, the classes are going to remain. The names will change and the misery is going to continue.

The question is very relevant, very meaningful, significant "What can I do with a beggar?" The beggar is not the question; the question is you and your heart. Do something, whatsoever you can do, and don't try to throw the responsibility on the rich. Don't try to throw the responsibility on history. Don't try to throw the responsibility on the economic structure, because that is secondary. If humanity remains cunning and calculative, it is

> "Unless the division between mind and heart is dissolved, unless humanity starts living through the heart and not through the mind, the classes are going to remain. The names will change and the misery is going to continue."

going to be repeated again and again and again.

What can you do about it? You are a small part of the total. Whatsoever you do will not change the situation – but it will change you. It may not change the beggar if you give something to him, but the very gesture, that you shared whatsoever you could, will change you. And that is important. And if this goes on – the revolution of the heart – people who feel, people who look at another human being as an end in itself... If this goes on increasing, one day the poor people will disappear, poverty will disappear. And it will not be replaced by a new category of exploitation.

> "It may not change the beggar if you give something to him, but the very gesture, that you shared whatsoever you could, will change you. And that is important."

Up to now all the revolutions have failed, because the revolutionaries have not been able to see the basic reason why there is poverty. They are looking only at superficial causes. Immediately they say, "Some people have exploited him, that's why this is possible. This is the cause; that's why there is poverty."

But why were some people able to exploit? Why could they not see? Why could they not see that they are gaining nothing and this man is losing all? They may accumulate wealth, but they are killing life all around. Their wealth is nothing but blood. Why can they not see it? The cunning mind has created explanations there, also. The cunning mind says. "People are poor because of their karma. In the past lives they have done something wrong, that's why they are suffering. I am rich because I have done good deeds, so I am enjoying the fruit." This is also the mind. Marx sitting in the British Museum is also a mind, and thinking about what is the basic cause of poverty, his mind comes to feel that there are people who exploit. But these people will be there always unless cunningness disappears completely. It is not a question of changing the structure of the society. It is a question of changing the whole structure of human personality.

What can you do? You can change, you can throw out the rich

people – they will come back from the back door. They were cunning. In fact, those who are doing the throwing are also very cunning; otherwise they cannot throw. The rich people may not be able to come from the back door, but the people who call themselves revolutionaries, communists, socialists – they will sit on the throne, and then they will start exploiting. And they will exploit more dangerously because they have proved themselves more cunning than the rich. By throwing out the rich, they have proved one thing absolutely, that they are more cunning than the rich. The society will be in the hands of more cunning people.

And remember, if someday some other revolutionaries are born – which are bound to be because again people will start feeling the exploitation is there; now it has taken a new form. Again there will be a revolution. But who will overthrow the past revolutionaries? Now even more cunning people will be needed. Whenever you are going to defeat a certain system, and you use the same means as the system has used for itself, just the names will change, the flags will change. The society will remain the same.

Enough of this befooling. The beggar is not the question, the question is you. Don't be cunning, don't be clever. Don't try to say that this is his karma – you don't know anything about karma. That is just a hypothesis to explain certain things which are unexplained, to explain certain things which cause heartache. Once you accept the hypothesis, you are relieved of the burden. Then you can remain rich and the poor can remain poor and there is no problem. The hypothesis functions as a buffer.

> "Whenever you are going to defeat a certain system, and you use the same means as the system has used for itself, just the names will change, the flags will change. The society will remain the same."

That's why in India poverty has remained so ingrained and people have become so insensitive toward it. They have a certain theory which helps them. It is just as you move in a car and the car has shock absorbers, the roughness of the road is not felt: the shock absorbers go on absorbing. This hypothesis of karma is a great shock absorber. You come up constantly against poverty, but there is a shock absorber – the theory of karma. What can you do? It has nothing to do with you. You are enjoying your riches because of your virtues – good deeds done in the past – and this man is suffering from his bad deeds.

There is in India a certain sect of Jainism, Terapanth. They are the extremist believers of this theory. They say, "Don't interfere because he is suffering his past karmas. Don't give him anything because that will be an interference. He could have suffered in a short time – you will be delaying the process. He will have to suffer." For example, you can give a poor man enough to live at ease for a few years, but again the suffering will start. You can give him enough to live at ease in this life, but again in the next life the suffering will start. Where you stopped his suffering, exactly from there, the suffering will start again. So those who believe in the Terapanth go on saying don't interfere. Even if somebody is dying by the side of the road, simply go on, indifferent, on your path. They say this is compassion; when you interfere you delay the process.

What a great shock absorber! In India people have become absolutely insensitive. A cunning theory protects them.

In the West they have found a new hypothesis: it is because the rich have exploited people, so destroy the rich. Just look at it. Looking at a poor man, love starts rising in your heart. You immediately say, "This poor man is poor because of the rich." You have turned love into hate – now hate arises toward the rich man. What game are you playing? Now you say, "Destroy the rich! Take everything back from them. They are the criminals." Now the beggar is forgotten; the heart is full of love no more. On the contrary, it is full of hate – and hate has created the society in which beggars exist! Now again hate is functioning in you. You will create a society in which categories may change, names may change, but there will be the ruled and the rulers, the exploited and the exploiters, the oppressors and the oppressed. It will not make much difference; it will remain the same. There will be masters and there will be slaves.

The only revolution possible is the revolution of the heart.

When you see a beggar, remain sensitive. Don't allow any shock absorber to come between you and the beggar. Remain sensitive. It is difficult because you will start crying. It is difficult because it will be very, very uncomfortable. Share whatsoever you can share. And don't be worried whether he will remain a beggar or not – you did whatsoever you could.

This will change you. This will give you a new being, closer to the heart and farther away from the mind. This is your inner transformation, and this is the only way. If individuals go on changing in this way, there may sometime arise a society where people are so sensitive that they cannot exploit, where people have become so alert and aware that they cannot oppress, where people have become so loving that just to think of poverty, of slavery, is impossible.

Do something out of the heart and don't fall a victim of theories. The questioner goes on:

> *You have said we must incorporate the opposite pole;*
> *we must choose both science and religion. Rationality*
> *and irrationality, West and East, technology and*
> *spirituality. Can I choose both politics and*
> *meditation? Can I choose to change the world and to*
> *change myself at the same time? Can I be a*
> *revolutionary and a sannyasin at once?*

Yes, I have said again and again that one has to accept the polarities. But meditation is not a pole. Meditation is the acceptance of the polarities, and through that acceptance one transcends beyond the polarities. So there is no opposite to meditation. Try to understand.

You are sitting in your room full of darkness. Is darkness the opposite of light, or just the absence of light? If it is opposite to light, then it has its own existence. Does darkness have its own existence? Is it real in its own way, or is it just the absence of light? If it has a reality of its own, then when you light a candle it will resist. It will try to put the candle out. It will fight for its own existence; it will resist. But it gives no resistance. It never fights, it can never put out a small candle. Vast darkness and a small candle, but the candle cannot be defeated by that vast darkness. The darkness may have ruled in that house for centuries, but you bring a small candle: the darkness cannot say, "I am centuries old and I will give a good fight." It simply disappears.

Darkness has no positive reality, it is simply the absence of light, so when you bring light it disappears. When you put the light off, it appears. In fact it never goes out and never comes in, because it cannot go out and cannot come in. Darkness is nothing but the absence of light. Light present, darkness is not there; light absent, it is there. It is absence.

Meditation is the inner light. It has no opposite, only absence.

The whole of life is an absence of meditation as you live it – the worldly life, the life of power, prestige, ego, ambition, greed. And that is what politics is.

Politics is a very big word. It does not include only the so-called politicians. It includes all the worldly people because whosoever is ambitious is a politician, whosoever is struggling to reach somewhere is a politician. Wherever there is competition there is politics. Thirty students studying in the same class and calling themselves "class fellows" – they are class enemies because they are all competing. Not "fellows" – they are all trying to overtake each other. They are all trying to get the gold medal, to come first. The ambition is there: they are already politicians. Wherever there is competition and struggle there is politics. So the whole of ordinary life is politics-oriented.

> *"If individuals go on changing in this way, there may sometime arise a society where people are so sensitive that they cannot exploit, where people have become so alert and aware that they cannot oppress, where people have become so loving that just to think of poverty, of slavery, is impossible."*

Meditation is like light. When meditation comes, politics disappears. So you cannot be meditative and political. That is impossible:

you are asking for the impossible. Meditation is not one pole; it is the absence of all conflict, all ambition, all ego-trips.

Let me tell you a very famous Sufi story. It happened:

A Sufi said, "None can understand man until he realizes the connection between greed, obligingness, and impossibility."

"This," said his disciple, "is a conundrum which I cannot understand."

The Sufi said, "Never look for understanding through conundrums when you can attain it through experience directly."

He took the disciple to a shop in the nearby market where robes were sold. "Show me your very best robe," said the Sufi to the shopkeeper, "for I am in a mood to spend excessively."

A most beautiful garment was produced, and an extremely high price was asked for it. "It is very much the kind of thing I would like," said the Sufi. "But I would like some sequins around the collar and a touch of fur trimming.

"Nothing easier," said the seller of the robes, "for I have just such a garment in the workroom of my shop." He disappeared for a few moments and then returned having added the fur and the sequins to the selfsame garment.

"And how much is this one?" asked the Sufi.

"Twenty times the price of the first one," said the shopkeeper.

"Excellent," said the Sufi. "I shall take both of them."

Now, the impossibility – because it is the selfsame garment. The Sufi was showing that greed has a certain impossibility in it; impossibility is intrinsic to greed.

Now, don't be too greedy because this is the greatest greed there is – to ask to be a politician and a meditator together simultaneously. That is the greatest greed possible. You are asking to be ambitious and non-tense. You are asking to fight, to be violent, to be greedy, and yet peaceful and relaxed. If it were possible then there would have been no need for sannyas; then there would have been no need for meditation.

You cannot have both. Once you start meditating, politics starts disappearing. And with politics, all the effects of politics also disappear. The tense state, the worry, the anxiety, the anguish, the violence, the greed – they all disappear. They are by-products of a political mind.

You will have to decide: either you can be a politician or you can be a meditator. You cannot be both because when meditation comes, the darkness disappears. This world, your world, is an absence of meditation. And when meditation comes, this world simply disappears like darkness.

That's why Patanjali, Shankara, and others who have known go on saying that this world is illusory, not real. Illusory like darkness: it appears to be real when it is there, but once you bring light in suddenly you become aware it was not real. It was unreal. Just look into darkness, how real it is! How real it looks, it is there surrounding you from everywhere. Not only that, you are feeling afraid. The unreal is creating fear. It can kill you, and it is not there!

Bring light. Keep somebody by the door to see whether or not he sees the darkness going out. Nobody ever sees darkness going out; nobody ever sees darkness coming in. It appears to be, and it is not.

The so-called world of desire and ambition, politics, only appears to be and it is not. Once you meditate you start laughing about the whole nonsense, the whole nightmare that has disappeared.

But please don't try to do this impossible thing. If you try, you will be in much conflict; you will become a split personality. "Can I choose both politics and meditation? Can I choose to change the world and to change myself at the same time?" Not possible.

In fact, you are the world. When you change yourself you have started to change the world – and there is no other way. If you start changing others you will not be able to change yourself, and one who is not able to change himself cannot change anybody. He can only go on believing that he is doing great work, as your politicians go on believing.

Your so-called revolutionaries are all ill people, tense people, mad people – insane – but their insanity is such that if they are left to themselves they will go completely mad, so they put their insanity into some occupation. Either they start changing the society, reforming the society, doing this and that, changing the whole world… And their madness is such, they cannot see the stupidity of it. You have not changed yourself – how can you change anybody else?

Start closer to home. First change yourself; first bring the light within yourself, then you will be capable…. In fact to say then there will be any capacity to change others is not right. In fact once you change yourself, you become a source of infinite energy, and that energy changes others on its own accord. Not that you go on and work hard and become a martyr in changing people, no – nothing of that sort. You simply remain in yourself, but the very energy, the purity of it, the innocence of it, the fragrance of it goes on spreading in ripples. It reaches all the shores of the world. Without any effort on your side, an effortless revolution starts. And the revolution is beautiful when it is effortless. When it is with effort it is violent; then you are forcing your ideas on somebody else.

Stalin killed millions of people because he was a revolutionary. He wanted to change the society, and whosoever was obstructing in any way had to be killed and removed. Sometimes it happens that those who are trying to help you start helping even against you. They don't bother whether you want to be changed or not; they have an idea to change you and they will change you in spite of you. They won't listen to you. This type of revolution is going to be violent, bloody.

And a revolution cannot be violent, cannot be bloody, because a revolution has to be a revolution of love and heart. A real revolutionary never goes anywhere to change anybody. He remains rooted in himself, and people who want to be changed come to him. They travel from faraway lands. They come to him. The fragrance reaches them. In subtle ways, in unknown ways, whosoever wants to change himself comes and seeks a revolutionary. The real revolutionary remains in himself, available. Like a pool of cool water – whosoever is thirsty will seek. The pool is not going to search for you; the pool is not going to run after you. And the pool is not going to drown you because you are thirsty, such that if you don't listen then the pool will drown you. Stalin killed so many people! Revolutionaries have been as violent as reactionaries, and sometimes even more so.

Please don't try to do the impossible. Just change yourself. In fact that too is such an impossibility that if you can change yourself in this life, you can feel grateful. You can say. "Enough, more than enough has happened." Don't be worried about others. They are also beings, they have consciousness, they have souls. If they want to change, nobody is hindering the path. Remain a pool of cool water. If they are thirsty they will come. Just your coolness will be the invitation; your purity of water will be the attraction.

"Can I be a revolutionary and a sannyasin at once?" No. If you are a sannyasin you are a revolution, not a revolutionary. You need not be a revolutionary.

If you are a sannyasin you are a revolution. Try to understand what I am saying. Then you don't go to change people, you don't go to create any revolution anywhere. You don't plan it – you live it. Your very style of life is revolution. Wherever you will look, wherever you will touch, there will be revolution. Revolution will become just like breathing, spontaneous.

Another Sufi story I would like to tell you:

A well-known Sufi was asked. "What is invisibility?"

He said, "I shall answer that when an opportunity for a demonstration occurs."

Sufis don't talk much. They create situations. They don't say much; they show through situations. So the Sufi said, "Whenever an opportunity occurs, I will give you a demonstration."

Sometime later, that man and the one who had asked him the question were stopped by a band of soldiers, and the soldiers said, "We have orders to take all dervishes into custody, for the king of this country says that they will not obey his commands and that they say things which are not welcome to the tranquility of thought of the populace. So we are going to imprison all the Sufis."

Whenever there is a really religious person, a revolution, the politicians become very much afraid because his very presence maddens them. His very presence is enough to create a chaos. His very presence is enough to create a disorder, a death to the old society. His very presence is enough to create a new world. He becomes a vehicle. Absent, completely absent as far as his ego is concerned, he becomes a vehicle of the divine. The rulers, the cunning people have always been afraid of religious people because there cannot be more danger than a religious person. They are not afraid of revolutionaries because their strategies are the same. They are not afraid of revolutionaries because they use the same language, their terminology is the same. They are the same people; they are not different people.

Just watch the politicians. All the politicians who are in power and all the politicians who are not in power – they are all the same people. Those who are in power seem to be reactionaries because they have attained power and now they want to protect it. Now they want to keep it in their hands, so they seem to be the establishment. Those who are not in power talk about revolution because they want to throw out those who are in power. Once they are in power they will become the reactionaries, and the people who were in power, who were thrown out of power, will become the revolutionaries.

A successful revolutionary is a dead revolutionary, and a ruler thrown out of his power becomes a revolutionary. And they go on deceiving the people. Whether you choose those who are in power or those who are not in power, you are not choosing different people. You are choosing the same people. They have different labels, but there is not a bit of difference.

A religious person is a real danger. His very being is dangerous, because he brings through him new worlds.

The soldiers surrounded the Sufi and his disciple, and they said they were in search of Sufis, that all Sufis have to be imprisoned because the king has commanded so, saying that they say things which are not welcome and they create such thought patterns which are not good for the tranquility of the populace.

And the Sufi said, to the soldiers, "And so you should, for you must do your duty."

"But are you not Sufis?" asked the soldiers.

"Test us." said the Sufi.

The officer took out a Sufi book. "What is this?" he said.

The Sufi looked at the title page and said, "Something which I will burn in front of you, since you have not already done so." He set fire to the book, and the soldiers rode away satisfied.

The Sufi's companion asked, "What was the purpose of that action?"

"To make us invisible," said the Sufi. "For to the man of the world, visibility means that you are looking like something or someone he expects you to resemble. If you look different, your true nature becomes invisible to him."

A religious man lives a life of revolution, but invisible – because to become visible is to become gross, to become visible is to come to the lowest rung of the ladder. A religious person, a sannyasin, creates a revolution in himself and remains invisible. And that invisible source of energy goes on doing miracles.

Please, if you are a sannyasin there is no need to be a revolutionary. You are already a revolution. And I say a revolution because a revolutionary is already dead, a revolutionary already has fixed ideas – a revolutionary already has a mind. I say revolution – it is a process. A sannyasin has no fixed ideas; he lives moment to moment. He responds to the reality of the moment, not out of fixed ideas.

Just watch. Talk to a Communist and you will see that he is not listening. He may be nodding his head, but he is not listening. Talk to a Catholic, he is not listening. Talk to a Hindu, he is not listening. While you are talking he is preparing his answer – from his old, past, fixed ideas. You can even see on the face that there is no response, a dullness and deadness. Talk to a child – the child listens, he listens attentively. If he listens at all, he listens attentively. If he does not listen then he is absolutely absent, but he is total! Talk to a child and you will see the response, pure and fresh. A sannyasin is like a child, innocent. He does not live out of his ideas: he is not a slave to any ideology. He lives out of consciousness, he lives out of awareness. He acts herenow. He has no yesterdays and he has no tomorrows, only today.

> *"All the politicians who are in power and all the politicians who are not in power – they are all the same people."*

When Jesus was crucified, a thief who was at his side said to him.

"We are criminals. We are crucified, that's okay – we can understand. You look innocent. But I am happy just to be crucified with you. I am tremendously happy. I have never done anything good."

He had completely forgotten something. When Jesus was born, Jesus' parents were escaping from the country because the king had ordered a mass murder of all the children born in a certain period. The king had come to know from his wise men that a revolution is going to be born, and there is going to be danger. It is better to prevent it beforehand, take precautions. So he had ordered a mass murder. Jesus' parents were escaping.

One night they were surrounded by a few thieves and robbers – this thief was one of that group – and they were going to rob and kill them. But this thief looked at the child Jesus, and he was so beautiful, so innocent, so pure, as if purity itself…and a certain glow was surrounding him. So he stopped the other thieves, and he said. "Let them go. Just look at the child." And they all looked at the child, and they all were in a certain hypnosis. They couldn't do what they wanted to do…and they left them.

This was the thief who had saved Jesus, but he was not aware that this is the same man. He said to Jesus, "I don't know what I have done, because I have never done a good deed. You cannot find a greater criminal than me. My whole life was that of sin – robbery, murder, and everything you can imagine. But I am happy. I am thankful to God that I am dying by the side of such an innocent man."

> *"A religious man lives not out of past ideologies, ideas, fixed concepts, philosophies. He lives in this moment."*

Jesus said. "Just because of this gratefulness, you will be in the kingdom of God with me today."

Now, after that statement, Christian theologians have been continuously discussing what he meant by "today." He simply meant now. Because a religious man has no yesterdays, no tomorrows, only today. This moment is all. When he said to the thief, "Today you will be with me in the kingdom of God," in fact he was saying,

"Look! You are already. This very moment, by your gratefulness, by your recognition of purity and innocence – by your repentance – the past has disappeared. We are in the kingdom of God."

A religious man lives not out of past ideologies, ideas, fixed concepts, philosophies. He lives in this moment. Out of his consciousness he responds. He is always fresh like a fresh spring, always fresh, uncorrupted by the past.

So, if you are a sannyasin, you are a revolution. A revolution is greater than all the revolutionaries. Revolutionaries are those who have stopped somewhere, the river has become frozen, it flows no more. A sannyasin is always flowing. The river never stops – it goes on and on, flowing and flowing. A sannyasin is a flow.

CHAPTER 5

Church and State

The politicians and the priests have a vested interest in keeping the people of the world unaware of the future. The reason is very simple: if the people are aware of the future and the darkness ahead, the death that is coming closer every moment, there is going to be a tremendous upheaval in the consciousness of man all around the world. And the politicians and the priests, who have dominated humanity for millennia, know perfectly well they cannot solve any problem that is going to be faced by humanity in the future. They are absolutely impotent. The problems are too big and they are too small. The only way for them to save their faces is not to let the people become aware of what is happening tomorrow.

I have to make it clear also that politics attracts only the most mediocre minds in the world. It does not attract Albert Einsteins, Bertrand Russells, Jean-Paul Sartres, Rabindranath Tagores... No, it attracts a certain kind of people. Psychologists are aware of the fact that people who are suffering from some inferiority complex are the people to be attracted toward politics, because politics can give them power. And through power they can convince themselves and others that they are not inferior, that they are not mediocre.

But just attaining power makes no difference to their intelligence.

So the whole world is ruled by mediocre people, when we have a large number of intelligent people – scientists, artists, musicians, poets, dancers, painters – all kinds of sensitive, creative people, the very cream of humanity, but they are not in power. They can change the whole fabric of human history, they can change the darkness of the future into a beautiful morning, a sunrise. But the misfortune is that power is in the hands of the wrong people, and the people of intelligence are devoid of power.

I will tell you a small story to make it clear:

A great mystic heard that one of his friends, a childhood friend – they had played together, studied together – had become the prime minister of the country. Just to congratulate him, the mystic came down from the mountains. It was a long journey, tiring. By the time he reached the prime minister's palace, the prime minister was getting ready to go somewhere.

He recognized the mystic, but he said, "I'm sorry, I have some appointments. I have to go to three places, and I would love it if you can come with me. On the way we can talk and remember the golden old days."

The mystic said, "I would love to come with you, but you can see my rags are full of dust. It would not look right to sit by your side on a golden chariot."

The prime minister said, "Don't be worried. The king has presented me with a very costly overcoat. I have never used it; I have been keeping it for some special occasion. I will give you the coat. Just put it on; it will cover your clothes, the dust and everything."

The coat was given to him. They reached the first house. They entered the house. The prime minister introduced his friend: "He is a great mystic. He lives in the mountains. Everything that he has is his own, except the coat – that is mine."

The mystic could not believe it: "What kind of stupidity is this?" Even the family was shocked, to insult the mystic in such a way.

Outside the house the mystic said, "It is better I do not accompany you. You insulted me. What was the need to say that it is your coat? They were not asking."

He said, "I am sorry, forgive me. And if you don't come with me to the next appointment, I will think you have not forgiven me."

The mystic was a simple-hearted man. He said, "Then it is okay, I am coming."

Entering the second house, the prime minister introduced him: "He is a great mystic who lives in the mountains. Everything is his – even the coat is his!"

The mystic could not believe that this man had any intelligence at all. Outside he simply refused: "I cannot go to your third appointment. This is too much."

But the politician said, "I have said that the coat is yours!"

The mystic said, "It is unbelievable how unintelligent a man can be. Your assertion, emphasis, that the coat is mine, creates suspicion: there is something you are hiding. What is the need to mention the coat at all? I don't see the point that in any introduction coats need to be introduced."

And the politician said, "Forgive me, but if you don't come to the third appointment I will never forget that I have hurt you. Please, there is only one more appointment, and I will not say that the coat is yours or the coat is mine. Don't be worried about it."

The simple mystic, innocent, agreed to go with him. At the third house he introduced the mystic in the same way, "He is a great mystic from the mountains. All the clothes are his, but as far as the coat is concerned, it is better not to say anything!"

The politician is not the most intelligent part of humanity. Otherwise there would not have been five thousand wars in three thousand years. The politician has destroyed, but has not created anything. It is the politician who is creating the atomic weapons, the nuclear missiles. With what face can he make the people of the world aware that the future is dark, dismal? Perhaps there is no future anymore, perhaps we are sitting on a volcano which can erupt any moment. Already we have so many nuclear weapons that we can destroy seven hundred planets of the size of our earth. In other words, we can kill every man seven hundred times over.

Can you think of the stupidity of it? A poor man simply dies one time; there is no need to kill him seven hundred times. For what is all this nuclear arrangement being made? There is a certain madness behind it. The madness is that the politician can live only if there is war.

In his autobiography, Adolf Hitler has made many significant statements. One of the statements is that if a politician wants to be a great hero, a great historical figure, then the only way is to create a great war. Without war you don't have heroes. Just think of all your heroes, they have been created by war: Alexander the Great, Napoleon Bonaparte, Nadirshah, Tamerlane, Genghis Khan, Joseph Stalin, Benito Mussolini, Adolf Hitler, Winston Churchill... And what have these people got, except that they lived at the time of a great war? The war brings them to the pinnacle of their glory. And your whole history is full of these idiots.

> "We have produced great poets. We have produced great painters. Our history should remember them. Our history should remind us that they are our real forefathers, not Genghis Khan, not Tamerlane, not Nadirshah."

If we have any sense, we should completely stop studying this kind of history in the schools and universities. Can't you study beautiful people, creative people? We have produced great musicians. We have produced great scientists. We have produced great poets. We have produced great painters. Our history should remember them. Our history should remind us that they are our real forefathers, not Genghis Khan, not Tamerlane, not Nadirshah. These are accidents, and they should not even have a place in the footnotes of history books. They should be simply ignored. They were mad people, and there is no need to go on studying them and creating the same kind of desire in the new generation.

The priests are also in a deep conspiracy with the politicians. It is a thousands-of-years-old conspiracy: the priest protects the politician; the politician protects the priest. It has to be understood.

For example, in the East the priest has been telling the people,

"You are poor because in your past life you have been doing evil acts." He has convinced people. When you go on saying the same thing again and again for thousands of years, it leaves an impression deep in the minds of people. Not only does it impress the people, it even impresses the priest himself! It is a very strange psychological phenomenon.

I am reminded of an anecdote:

A journalist died. He reached directly to the door of paradise and knocked on the door. A small window opened and the door-keeper said, "Forgive me, we have a certain quota for journalists that is complete. We need only one dozen journalists in paradise. In fact, even they are useless, because nothing happens here – no news."

Just remember the definition of news: when a dog bites a man, it is not news; when a man bites a dog, it is news. And naturally in paradise there is no news.

"Even the twelve journalists are getting bored, so please go to the other door, in front."

But journalists are stubborn people, you cannot get rid of them so easily. He said, "Just listen to this one thing. I will go to the other door after twenty-four hours, but not now."

The doorkeeper said, "What will you do for twenty-four hours, standing here?"

He said, "I am not going to stand here, you can let me in. If I can convince one of the twelve journalists to go to hell, then you can give me his place. The quota will remain complete."

Even the doorkeeper thought that was sensible. He said, "Okay, come in. Have a try."

After twenty-four hours he managed to tell everybody, journalists, non-journalists, "In hell there is going to be a new newspaper published which will be the largest and the most important. They need editors, subeditors, reporters, all kinds of journalists – with great salaries!"

After twenty-four hours he went back to the gate. The gate-keeper said, "You cannot get out."

He asked, "What do you mean?"

The doorkeeper said, "All twelve have escaped. You convinced them, and they were creating so much fuss that I finally allowed them to go. Now you cannot leave, at least we should have one journalist."

But the journalist said, "I cannot stay."

The doorkeeper said, "You created the lie. There is no newspaper. There are no great salaries."

He said, "Yes, I created the lie, but if twelve people have believed it there must be something to it! I don't want to be here. Open the door, otherwise I am going to complain. I don't belong here, I'm not supposed to be here." Seeing the point that it was true, the doorkeeper allowed him to go without permission from any higher authority.

What had happened to the journalist? He had invented a lie, and he succeeded in convincing twelve people. Whenever you convince somebody, you are also being convinced simultaneously.

For centuries in the East the priesthood has been convincing people that it is your past evil acts which have made you poor. All you need to do is to remain contented with your poverty, with your sickness, with your death. This is a test of your trust. And if you can pass through this fire test, in the next life, after death, you will be rewarded enormously. This is the reason that in the East science has not progressed, technology has not been born. If poor people are contented, if the poor people don't want to be anything other than poor, then what is the need of technology, of science, of progress, of evolution, of creating more wealth, of creating a better society, of distributing the wealth in a more human way? There is no need.

> "The priest protects the politician against the revolution."

The politician is happy, because there is no possibility of revolution. The priest protects the politician against the revolution. And the politician, on his part, goes on praising the priest, that he is a great saint. He touches the feet of the priest, particularly at the time of elections. He gives respect; he goes to all kinds of saints, *shankaracharyas*, imams, popes. Soon the pope is going to come to

India, and you will see all the politicians running to welcome him –
now in India, Christianity is the third largest religion. Now the pope
has to be persuaded. Mohammedan saints, dead or alive, have to be
worshipped. Hindu saints, whether saints or simply idiots, have to
be raised to the highest spirituality.

This is a conspiracy to exploit the people. The priests cannot say
what is going to happen in the future, for the simple reason that the
priest lives out of the past. He lives out of the Shrimad Bhagavadgita,
which happened five thousand years ago. He lives by the Koran
Sharif, he lives by the Holy Bible. His whole world is in the past; he
is a worshipper of the dead. He has no eyes for the future, and
no intelligence either. I don't think any man of intelligence can be
a priest, because the priest is continuously lying, and no man of
integrity can do that.

The priest is lying on every count. He knows nothing of God.
He has not experienced, he has not encountered, but he goes on
lying to the people – pretending to be a representative of God, a
mediator between you and God. He does not allow you to be in
direct contact with existence. He always wants you to write your
love letters "care of" the priest. Your prayers can reach God only
through the priest. Strange, on what authority…?

The head of the Christians, the Polack pope, declared that one
of the greatest sins is to confess directly to God – confession has to
be to the priest. Do you understand this cunning strategy? The
Catholic priest is always there to listen to your confession, and you
have to tell him everything about your sins, your private life. That
gives him power. Do you understand? He has a file on you. You
cannot leave the Catholic fold. He can expose you. He can destroy
your respectability. He knows that you have had a love affair
with your neighbor's wife…. You can hide from everybody but not
from the priest, because he is the only one who can manage forgive-
ness from God for your sins.

But strange, why can you not confess to God directly? This is
politics; this is not religion.

I have come across priests of all the religions, and I have never
seen any one of them that has any intelligence. If they had any

intelligence they would compose music, they would create some beauty, they would invent something to enhance humanity. They would find some way to destroy poverty in the world. But the priest goes on doing just the contrary. All the priests of all the religions, without exception, are against birth control, they are against abortion. I was talking to a bishop and I told him that if there are abortions, he was responsible for them.

He said, "What are you saying? We are against abortion."

I said, "Yes, I know it, but you are also against birth control. If you were in favor of birth control there would be no need for abortions."

Seeing the whole world growing in population and poverty, these priests go on teaching that children are produced by God, and that to prevent more births by any scientific method is against religion. I cannot think that these people are intelligent. They want to turn the whole earth into an Ethiopia. Millions of people will die by the end of this century without any nuclear weapons being used. Almost half of the earth will die of starvation. And when fifty percent of the people are dying in the streets and you cannot do anything to help – no medicine, no food, you cannot even arrange for their bodies to be carried to the graveyard or to the funeral pyre – the people who are left alive will be in a far more miserable condition than those who are dead. The dead will be the fortunate ones. Who will be responsible for all this? All these priests.

> *"Religions are interested in increasing their population, because population is power."*

I have been saying to all these priests, "Just look! If God, according to you, according to all religions, is omnipotent, all powerful, he can do anything. He can create the world, he can destroy the world. So what is the problem? The woman has just taken a pill – he cannot destroy a pill! If he wants the child to be born, the pill will be destroyed. The pill seems to be more powerful than your omnipotent God. You should go to your churches and temples and mosques and synagogues, and pray to God to destroy all the pills. You trust and believe in prayer – why are you harassing the poor people and telling them to continue to produce children?"

Religions are interested in increasing their population, because population is power. They are not worried about the death that is coming closer every moment. Politicians are interested in having more and more powerful weapons, because without nuclear weapons they are not going to be historical heroes. Even poor countries who need food are trying to make atomic plants, nuclear weapons plants. It seems to be an utterly insane state of affairs.

If we want a sane world, if we want to save the world, my humble suggestion is that there should be a world academy of scientists, of painters, of poets, of dancers, of sculptors, of architects, of professors, of mystics, and they should create public opinion. The intelligentsia of the world, from all dimensions and all sections, together should create a great public opinion: "We want to know exactly the truth. What is our future? What are the politicians going to do about changing it? What are the priests going to do? And if they are impotent, then they should simply say that, because there are people of merit who can do something."

Just a few days ago twenty American scientists, their best nuclear experts, protested to the government saying, "If you don't listen to us, we are going to stop working. We cannot work against the whole of humanity." Now this is a good beginning. The same should be done in every country. The same should be done in every part of the world, and why should you do it separately? It should be done together. All the intelligent scientists and creative people of the world should be together, because the question is very big. And unless every intelligent person is standing up to save humanity it seems to be an impossible task.

But I am not a pessimist, I hope even against hope. I feel that in times of challenge there is always a possibility of the best coming up, of people joining hands together across the foolish boundaries of politics that do not exist on the earth, against the boundaries of religions that are not religious at all. To be religious you need not be a Christian, you need not be a Hindu, you need not be a Mohammedan. To be a scientist, do you need to be a Hindu? Do you need to be a Christian? Religion is the science of the inner soul. There is no need for any adjective.

Just as science explores the objective existence, religion explores the interiority of man, his subjectivity. A man can be religious without being in any fold, and this is the time to declare, "I do not belong to any religion and yet I am religious. I do not belong to any nation and yet I am a human being. The whole earth is mine."

It is time that the whole humanity stands together against all conspiracies of the priests and the politicians. And I guarantee you that we can save humanity – not only save it, we can transform it into a higher form, into a better consciousness.

We can give birth to a new man.

The old man is finished.

Politics, for centuries, has been just killing, destroying people – the whole history of politics is the history of criminals, murderers. In three thousand years, politicians have created five thousand wars. It seems that inside the politician, the barbarous instinct is very powerful; its only joy is to destroy, to dominate.

> "I do not belong to any religion and yet I am religious. I do not belong to any nation and yet I am a human being. The whole earth is mine."

Religion creates a problem for it, because religion has given to the world its highest peaks of consciousness – a Gautam Buddha, a Jesus, a Chuang Tzu, a Nanak, a Kabir. These are the very salt of the earth. What has politics given to the world? Genghis Khan? Tamerlane? Nadir Shah? Alexander? Napoleon? Ivan the Terrible? Josef Stalin? Adolf Hitler? Benito Mussolini? Mao Zedong? Ronald Reagan? These are all criminals. Rather than being in power, they should be behind bars; they are inhuman.

They are spiritually sick people. The will to power and to dominate arises only in the sick mind. It arises out of the inferiority complex. People who are not suffering from an inferiority complex do not care about power; their whole endeavor is for peace because the meaning of life can be known only in peace – power is not the way. Peace, silence, gratitude, meditation – these are the basic constituents of religion.

Religion cannot be allowed to be dominated by stupid politicians. The situation is as if sick people are trying to dominate the physicians, directing what they should do and what they should not do. Accept it – the sick people are in the majority, but that does not mean that the physician should be dominated by the majority. The physician can heal the wounds, can cure the sicknesses of humanity. Religion is the physician.

Politicians have done enough harm, and they are leading the whole of humanity toward a global suicide: the whole of life on this planet is in danger. Not only man but the innocent birds and their songs, the silent trees and their flowers – everything that is alive. Politicians have managed to create enough destructive powers to destroy life on the earth; and they are continually piling up more and more nuclear weapons. In fact, three years ago there were enough nuclear weapons to destroy every man seven times, to destroy this whole earth seven times, or to destroy seven earths – although a man dies only once. There is no need to accumulate so much destructive power. The whole of politics depends on lies.

Politicians live on lies; politicians live on promises – but those promises are never fulfilled. They are the most unqualified people in the world. Their only quality is that they can manage to befool the poor masses – or, in poor countries, they can purchase their votes. And once they are in power, they forget completely that they are servants of the people; they start behaving as if they are the masters of the people.

As far as I can see, all politicians should be meditators, should know something of the inner world. They should be more conscious, more compassionate, should know the taste of love. They should know the experience of the silence of existence, and the beauty of this planet, and the gifts of existence. And they should learn to be humble and grateful.

Religion should be the teacher of all the politicians. Unless politicians have something of religiousness, there is no future for humanity. The politicians are blind, they don't have eyes; they are deaf. They don't have a silent mind to listen to the truth.

The politician lives on war, lives on creating riots, lives on disturbance – these are his nourishment. Adolf Hitler has written in his autobiography: "Unless you have enemies, you cannot become a great leader. Even if you don't have enemies, create the fiction that your country is in danger, because when people are afraid they are ready to become slaves. When people are afraid they are ready to follow politicians."

> "Politicians live on lies; politicians live on promises – but those promises are never fulfilled."

Although he was an insane person, once in a while he made statements which are very significant. He has said, "The greatest leaders of humanity are born in times of war." So unless there is a great war, you cannot be a great leader; just to fulfill the desire of being a great leader, you have to kill millions of people. And he is right: in days of peace, people don't need to follow; people don't make the leader almost a god, so that his word becomes the law.

Politicians try in every way to keep countries afraid. China is gathering nuclear weapons on its boundary with India; Pakistan is gathering armies on its boundary with India – the Indian politicians go on insisting this is so. In Pakistan, they go on insisting that India is gathering armies on its boundary; in China, they go on insisting that India is preparing nuclear weapons. In the parliaments, they go on saying, "We are not creating anything" – but that is an absolute lie. The Chinese leader has to keep the people of China afraid. The Indian leader has to keep the Indian people afraid. The Pakistani leaders have to keep the Pakistani people afraid. In your fear is their power. The more afraid they make you, the more powerful they are. Outside the country they go on creating fictions, and inside the country they also continue: Hindu and Moham-medan riots, riots between Hindi-speaking and non-Hindi-speaking people. They want you to continue fighting for anything – any trivial thing. If you are engaged in fighting, they are in power. If you stop fighting, their power disappears. This is an ugly game.

It is one of the duties of religious people to keep themselves above politics and lead the people toward creative values, toward more humanity. In fact, if religions understand one thing – that the whole of humanity is one, and there is no need for any nations – all these pygmy politicians will disappear.

Only a religious man with clarity of vision, who does not need the votes of the people, can say the truth. Politicians can only say beautiful lies, consoling lies, just to get your votes. The religious man has nothing to get from you; on the contrary, speaking the truth can be dangerous to his life – it has always been so. Whenever truth is spoken, the man who has spoken it has been crucified. Politicians need power, not crucifixion. The world needs more religious people who are ready to say the truth even if it means crucifixion. The religious man is not afraid of being crucified for the simple reason that he knows there is no death. At the most they can destroy his body – but his consciousness, his soul, his godliness within, will go on living.

Religion should have a higher status, and religious people should be listened to. Parliament should continually invite religious people to give them ideas on how to solve the problems of the country, because they themselves seem to be absolutely impotent in solving anything. Problems go on growing. But the ego of the politician wants nobody to be higher than him. But whether you want it or not, the religious person is higher than you. You cannot bring transformation into people's consciousness – he can.

Certainly, religion should not step down from its sacredness into the trivial matters of politics. So I agree with this point: religion and politics should remain separate. The distance is big. Religion is a star in the sky and the politicians are creatures crawling on the earth. They are separate; there is no question that they should be separate. But politicians should remember that they are functioning in mundane matters, and that is not the true goal of humanity.

Religious people are making every effort to raise humanity – its consciousness, its love, its compassion – to a point where wars become impossible, where politicians cannot deceive people, where their lies and their promises can be exposed. This is not interfering with politics – this is simply protecting people from the exploitation of politicians.

Politics is something that belongs to the gutters. Religion belongs to the open, clean sky – just like a bird on the wing, flying across the sun to reach to the very center of existence. Certainly religious people cannot be participants in politics; but politicians should learn to be humble – their power should not make them blind. Power corrupts and absolute power corrupts absolutely; and all politicians are corrupted by their power. And what power do they have? Because they can kill you, their power is the power of a butcher – nothing glorious, respectable.

The religious man has a totally different quality of power. It is in his presence; it is in his great love and reverence for life; it is in his gratitude to existence. We should not forget that the lower should remain within its own limits. And the wise people of the country should be asked to address the parliament as often as possible on problems which politicians cannot solve, and don't even have the brains to solve.

Politicians should learn and listen to the advice of the religious people. The problems are so small that any man of intelligence and good will can easily solve them. But the politician does not want to solve them; he only talks about solving them because his power is dependent on how many problems you have. The more problems you have, the more miserable you are, the more powerful he is.

To the religious consciousness, the more joyful you are, the more loving, the more rejoicing... He wants your life to be a song and to be a dance. That is the only way we should worship the source of life – with our joy, with our songs, and with our dances.

Is it possible for a politician to be a religious man or for a religious man to be a politician?

It is absolutely impossible for a political man to be religious, because the ways of politics and religion are diametrically opposite. You have to understand that it is not a question of adding something to your personality – religion is not an addition. If you are political, you can be a painter, you can be a poet, you can be a musician – those are additions.

Politics and music are not diametrically opposite; on the contrary, music may help you to be a better politician. It will be relaxing, it will help you to get unburdened of the whole day and the anxieties that a politician has to go through. But religion is not an addition; it is a diametrically opposite dimension. So first you have to understand the political man, exactly what it means.

The political man is a sick man, psychologically sick, spiritually sick. Physically he may be perfectly okay. Usually politicians are physically okay; their whole burden falls on their psyche. You can see that. Once a politician loses his power he starts losing his physical health. Strange, when he was in power, he was so burdened with many anxieties and tensions, but he was physically perfect.

The moment power has gone, all the anxieties have also gone; now they will be somebody else's business. His psyche is unburdened, and in that unburdening all his sickness falls on his body. The politician suffers, as far as his physiology is concerned, only when he loses power; otherwise politicians tend to live long, and are physically well. Strange, but the reason is that their whole sickness is taken by their psyche, and when the psyche takes on the whole sickness, then the body can live unburdened. But if the psyche releases all its sickness, where is it going to go? Lower than the psychic is your physical existence – all sickness falls onto the body. Politicians out of power die very soon. Politicians in power live very long. It is a known fact, but the cause is not well known.

> "The political man is psychologically sick, and psychological sickness tends to become spiritual sickness when it becomes too much."

So the first thing to be understood is that the political man is psychologically sick, and psychological sickness tends to become spiritual sickness when it becomes too much, when the psyche cannot hold it any more. Now, be careful: if the politician is in power, then his psychic sickness is bound to spread to his spiritual being, because he is holding his psychic sickness so it does not fall downward. It is his power, he thinks it is his treasure; he won't allow it to fall down.

I am calling it sickness. To him it is his whole ego trip. He is living for it; there is no other purpose for him. So, when he is in power he holds his sickness tightly, but he does not know anything about the spiritual realm, so those doors are open. He cannot close those doors; he has no idea that there is something more than his mind. When he is in power, if his psychological sickness is too much, after a certain point it overflows his psyche and reaches his spirituality.

If he is out of power, he tends not to hold all that stupidity. Now he knows what it was, now he is aware that it was nothing worth holding. And anyway there is nothing to hold; the power has gone, he is a nobody.

Out of desperation, he relaxes – perhaps I should say, relaxation comes to him automatically. Now he can sleep, he can go for a morning walk. He can gossip, he can play chess; he can do anything. Psychically he finds himself loosening. The doors that he had kept closed between his psyche and the body start opening, and his body is bound to suffer now: he may have a heart attack, he may get any kind of sickness; anything is possible. His psychic sickness will flow to the weakest part of his body. But in power it flows upward, toward his being, of which he is unaware.

And what is the sickness? The sickness is the inferiority complex. Anybody who is interested in power is suffering from an inferiority complex; deep down he feels himself worthless, inferior to others.

And certainly in many ways everybody is inferior. You are not a Yehudi Menuhin, but there is no need to feel inferior because you never tried to be, and that is not your business. Yehudi Menuhin is not you either; so what is the problem, where is the conflict?

But the political mind suffers from a wound of inferiority and the politician goes on scratching the wound. Intellectually he is not an Albert Einstein – he compares himself with giants – psychologically he is not a Sigmund Freud. If you compare yourself with the giants of humanity you are bound to feel completely shrunk, worthless.

This worthlessness can be removed in two ways: one is religion;

the other is politics. Politics does not really remove it, it only covers it. It is the same sick man, the same man who was feeling inferior, who sits as a president. But just sitting on a chair as the president, what difference can it make to your inner situation?

The ego is so subtle and so slippery. And the politician is sick because of his ego. Now there are two ways: either he can cover the wound by becoming a president, a prime minister. He can cover the wound, but the wound is there. You can deceive the whole world but how can you deceive yourself? You know it. It is there; you have covered it.

The same is the situation of the politician: just pus, wounds, inferiority, feeling worthless.

Yes, he had reached higher and higher, and on each step of the ladder, the hope was that on the next step the wound would be healed. Inferiority creates ambition, because ambition simply means an effort to prove yourself superior.

There is no other meaning to ambition but an effort to prove yourself superior. But why make an effort to prove yourself superior unless you are suffering from inferiority?

I have never voted in my life. My uncles, my two uncles – I have two uncles who were in the freedom struggle – have been in jail. Neither of them could complete his education because they were caught and imprisoned. One uncle was just here for the festival. He was just in his matriculation class when he was caught, because he was part of a conspiracy to destroy a train, to bomb a bridge. They were making a bomb – and he was a student of chemistry, so he used to bring from the chemistry lab things needed to make the bomb. He was caught when he was just going to take the examination, just ten days before. And his education was finished because after three years when he came back, it was too late to start again. So he went into business. My elder uncle was in his BA final when he got caught, because he was also part of a conspiracy group against the government. My whole family was political, except my father. So they were all asking me, "Why don't you register, why don't you vote, and why are you wasting your energies? If you move in the direction of politics you can become the president of the country, you can become the premier of the country."

I said, "You have completely forgotten with whom you are talking. I don't suffer from any inferiority, so why should I be interested in becoming the president of the country? Why should I waste my life in becoming the president of the country? It is almost as if I have no cancer and you want me to be operated on for cancer – it is strange. Why should I be operated on unnecessarily? You suffer from some inferiority complex, and you are projecting your inferiority complex on me. I am perfectly okay as I am. I am absolutely grateful to existence wherever I am. Today, whatsoever happens is good. More than that I have never asked, so there is no way to disappoint me."

They said, "You talk of strange things. What is this inferiority complex and what has this inferiority complex to do with politics?"

I said, "You don't understand simple psychology and neither do your great politicians understand simple psychology."

All these politicians on top in the world are sick people, so one way is to go on covering their wounds. Yes, they can deceive others. When Jimmy Carter smiles you are deceived, but how can Jimmy Carter deceive himself? He knows it is just an exercise of the lips. There is nothing else inside, no smile. People reach the highest rung of the ladder; then they become aware that their whole life has been a wastage. They have arrived, but where? They have arrived at the place for which they had been fighting – and it was not a small fight; it was tooth and nail – and destroying so many people, using so many people as means, and stepping on their heads.

You have arrived at the last rung of the ladder but what have you gained? You have simply wasted your whole life. Now to even accept that needs tremendous courage. It is better to go on smiling and go on keeping the illusion: at least others believe that you are great. You know who you are. You are exactly the same as you were – perhaps worse, because all this struggle, all this violence has made you worse. You have lost all your humanity. You are no longer a being.

It is so far away from you, that Gurdjieff used to say that not every person has a soul, for the simple reason – not that it is literally true, but he used to say – "Not everybody has got a soul, only a very few people who discover their being have." They have it; others are simply living in the illusion, because scriptures say, and all the religions preach, that you are born with a soul. Gurdjieff was very drastic. He said, "It is all nonsense. You are not born with a soul. You have to earn it; you have to deserve it." And I can understand what he means, although I will not say that you are not born with a soul.

> "All these politicians on top in the world are sick people."

You are born with a soul, but that soul is only a potential, and whatsoever Gurdjieff is saying is exactly the same. You have to bring that potential to actuality. You have to earn it. You have to deserve it.

The politician recognizes it when his whole life has gone down the drain. Now, either he has to confess – which seems very stupid because he is confessing that his whole life has been the life of an idiot…

Wounds are not healed by covering them. Religion is a cure. The word *meditation* and the word *medicine* come from the same root. Medicine is for the body; what medicine is for the body, meditation is for the soul. It is medicinal, it is a cure.

You ask me, can a politician be religious? Remaining a politician, it is impossible. Yes, if he drops politics, then he is no longer a politician; he can become a religious man. So I am not dividing, not preventing the politician from becoming religious. What I am saying is: as a politician, he cannot be religious because those are two different dimensions.

Either you cover your wound or you cure it. You can't do both together. And to cure it you have to uncover it, not cover it. Uncover it, know it, go deep into it, suffer it.

What is needed is an exploration of your whole being, unprejudiced, without condemnation, because you will find many things which you have been told are bad, evil. So don't shrink back, let them be. You simply need not condemn them. You have started on an exploration. Just note that something is there, note it, and go on. Don't condemn it; don't name it. Don't bring any prejudice against or for, because that's what prevents you from exploring. Your inner world closes immediately, you become tense – something evil. You go inside and you see something, and you become afraid that it is evil: greed, lust, anger, jealousy. My God! All these things, in me – it is better not to go in.

That's why millions of people don't go in. They simply sit on the staircase outside their house. They live on the porch their whole life. It is a porch life! They never open the door of their house. And the house has many chambers; it is a palace. If you go in, you will come across many things which others have told you are wrong. You don't know, you simply say, "I am an ignorant man. I don't know who you are. I have just come to explore, to do a survey." And a surveyor need not be bothered about what is good and what is bad, he simply goes on looking, watching, observing.

And you will be surprised by the strangest experience: that what you have called love up to now, hidden just behind it is hate; just take note. What you have been saying up to now is humbleness, just behind it is hidden your ego; just take note.

If somebody asks me, "Are you a humble man?" I cannot say I am, because I know humbleness is only the ego standing on its head. I am not an egoist, how can I be humble?

Do you understand me? It is impossible to be humble without having an ego. And once you have seen that both are together, the strangest thing happens, as I was telling you. The moment you see your love and your hate, your humbleness and ego, are one, they evaporate. You have not to do anything at all. You have seen their secret. That secret was helping them to remain in you. You have seen the secret, now there is no place for them to hide.

Go in again and again, and you will find fewer and fewer things there. Gatherings inside you are withering; crowds are going away. And the day is not far off when you will be left alone, and there is nobody, emptiness is in your hands. And suddenly you are cured.

Don't compare at all, because you are you, and somebody else is somebody else. Why should I compare myself with Yehudi Menuhin or with Pablo Picasso? I don't see the point at all. They are doing their thing; I am doing my thing. They are enjoying doing their thing, perhaps – because about them I cannot be certain. But I am certain about myself that I am enjoying whatsoever I am doing or not doing.

Only about myself can I be certain. I know that if you go on exploring your inner world without condemnation, without appreciation, without thinking at all, just watching the facts, they start disappearing. A day comes, you are left alone, the whole crowd has gone away; and in that moment, for the first time you feel

> *"Don't compare at all, because you are you, and somebody else is somebody else."*

what psychic healing is. And from psychic healing the door opens to spiritual healing. You need not open it, it opens on its own. You just reach the psychic center and the door opens.

It has been waiting for you, perhaps for many lives. When you come, the door immediately opens, and from that door you not only see yourself, you see the whole of existence, all the stars, the whole cosmos.

Hence I can say absolutely: no politician can become religious unless he drops politics. Then he is not a politician, and what I am saying does not refer to him.

You have also asked: can a religious man become a politician? That is even more impossible than the first because there is no reason at all for him to become one. If inferiority is the cause that drives you into ambition, then how can a religious man become a politician? There is no driving force. But once in a while it has happened in the past, and it may happen in the future, so let me say this to you.

In the past it was possible because the world was dominated by the monarchy. Once in a while, the king's son might turn out to be a poet. It is very difficult for a poet to become the president of America; who is going to listen to him? People think he is crazy, and he will look like a hippie. He cannot shape up himself, and he is trying to shape up the whole world? But in the past it was possible because of the monarchy.

The last emperor of India, from whom the British took over, was

a poet – that is why the British could take over India – Bahadurshah
Zafar, one of the greatest Urdu poets. Now it is not possible for a
poet to become an emperor; it was just accidental that he was born
a son of an emperor.

The enemy forces were entering the capital and he was writing
poetry. When his prime minister knocked on the door and said, "It
is absolutely urgent, because the enemies have entered the capital,"
Bahadurshah said, "Don't disturb me. I am writing just the last four
lines. I think I will be able to finish these four lines before they come
here. Don't disturb." And he started writing. He finished his poem;
that was more important to him.

And he was such a simple and good man; he came out and he
said, "What is this nonsense of killing people? If you want the
country you take it, what is the fuss about? I was burdened with all
the anxieties, now you can be burdened with all the anxieties. Leave
me alone."

But they would not leave him alone because they were politicians and generals. To leave this man in New Delhi was dangerous:
he may collect his forces, he may have resources – nobody knows.
They took him from India into Burma; he died in Rangoon. In his
last poem, which he wrote from his deathbed, he said, "How poor I
am. I cannot get even six feet in my beloved's street." He is talking
about New Delhi, which he loved, which he had created; and he
was a poet so he made the city as beautiful as possible. He said, "I
cannot get even six feet to be buried in my own beloved's street.
How unfortunate Zafar" – Zafar was his poetic name – "How unfortunate, Zafar, you are."

He was buried in Rangoon; they did not even bring his dead
body to New Delhi. He insisted, "At least when I am dead take my
body to my city, to my country. A dead body cannot be dangerous."
But politicians and generals think in different ways. Bahadurshah
was the emperor loved by the people. Seeing him dead, "There may
be a revolt, there may be some trouble. Why get into trouble?
Bury him there in Rangoon. Nobody will even hear for years that he
has died."

So, in the old monarchical days, it was possible that in the western hemisphere a man like Marcus Aurelius could happen. He was a religious man, but this was just accidental. Marcus Aurelius could not become a president or a prime minister today because he would not go asking for votes; he would not beg – for what?

In India it happened a few times. Ashoka, one of the great emperors of India, was a religious man. He was so religious that when his son asked – the only son, who was going to be the successor – to become a monk, he danced. He said, "This is what I have been waiting for, that one day you would understand." Then his daughter, his only daughter – he had only two children, one son and one daughter – when the daughter, Sanghamitra, asked him – she also wanted to go into the world of meditation – he said, "Go. This is my only happiness." But today it is impossible.

In India there was one great king, Poras; he fought against Alexander the Great. And you will be surprised at how Western books have been unfair to this man Poras. Alexander the Great becomes a pygmy before Poras. When they reached India, Alexander played a trick – he was a politician...

Alexander sent his wife to meet Poras, on a particular day. There is a day in India, the day of the sisters, when the sister just binds a thread on your wrist. You may be her real brother, you may not be her real brother, but the moment she binds the thread on your wrist you become a brother to her. And it is a double oath: the brother says, "I will protect you," and the sister says, "I will pray for your protection."

On that particular day, Alexander sent his wife to Poras. He was staying outside Poras' kingdom. There is a river that was the boundary; he was staying outside, and he sent his wife. And when it was declared in Poras' court, "The wife of Alexander the Great wants to meet you," he came out to greet her, because in India that was a tradition. Even if the enemy comes to your home, he is a guest, and the guest is a god.

He took her into his court, gave her a throne to sit on, and said, "You could have called me. There was no need for you to come such a long way."

She said, "I have come to make you my brother. I have no brother and today, I heard, is the sisters' day; I could not resist."

This was a political game. And Poras could understand what Alexander and his wife understood about sisters' day, and why Alexander waited up to this day to send his wife, but he said, "This is perfectly right. If you don't have any brother, I am your brother." She had brought the thread; she tied it and Poras touched her feet. The brother has to touch the feet of the sister; whether she is younger or older does not matter.

A tremendous respect for womanhood has been there, side by side with a tremendous bitterness against women. Perhaps the bitterness was created by the monks and the priests, and the respect was created by the religious people. Immediately Alexander's wife said, "Now you are my brother, and I hope you will save me, but the only way to save me is not to kill Alexander. Would you like your sister to remain a widow all her life?"

Poras said, "There is no question about it. You need not speak about it – it is settled. Alexander will not be touched at all. Now we are related."

And this happened: the next day Alexander attacked, and a moment came in the fight when Poras killed Alexander's horse. Alexander fell from the horse and Poras was on his elephant – because in India, the elephant was the real fighter's animal, not the horse – the elephant was just going to put his feet on Alexander, and he would have been finished. Just by habit Poras pulled out his spear and was going to kill Alexander, when he saw the thread on his wrist. He put his spear back, told the mahout, the man who guides the elephant, "Move away, and inform Alexander that I will not kill him."

That was the moment when Alexander would have been killed, and all his desire for conquering the world would have been finished; the whole of history would have been different. But Poras was a religious man, made of a different mettle: ready to be defeated but not ready to be demoralized. And he was defeated – he missed his chance.

Poras was brought before Alexander in his court, a temporary court, with chains on his hands and his legs. But the way he walked…

Even Alexander said to him, "You are still walking like an emperor, even with chains on your feet and chains on your hands."

Poras said, "This is my way of walking. It has nothing to do with my being an emperor or a prisoner; this is my way of walking. This is how I am."

Alexander asked him, "How would you like to be treated?"

Poras said, "What a question! An emperor should be treated like an emperor. What a stupid question."

Alexander says in his notes, "I have never come across a man like Poras. He was in chains, imprisoned – I could have killed him immediately, then and there – but the way he walked, the way he talked…" Alexander was really impressed. He said, "Take away his chains; he will remain an emperor anywhere. Give his kingdom back to him. But," he said, "before we leave, I would like to ask you one question. When the chance was there when you could have killed me, why did you pull your spear back? Just one more second and I'd have been finished, or your elephant could have crushed me, but you prevented it. Why?"

Poras said, "Don't ask that. You know; you are a politician, I am not. This thread – do you recognize it? You had sent this thread with your wife; now she is my sister and I cannot kill my own brother-in-law. It is not possible for me to make her a widow. I chose to be defeated rather than to kill you. But there is no need for you to feel obliged toward me; this is just how a really centered man should behave."

So in the past it was possible because of the monarchy. But within the monarchy, idiots also became kings, madmen also became kings; everything is possible. So I am not supporting monarchy, I am simply saying that it was possible within the monarchy for a religious man, by accident, to become an emperor.

In the future, democracy is not going to last long because the politician is already ignorant before the scientist; he is already in the hands of the scientist. The future belongs to the scientist, not to the politician. That means we will have to change the word *democracy*. I have a word for it: *meritocracy*.

Merit will be the decisive factor. Not whether you can gather votes by canvassing all kinds of promises and hopes, but your merit, your real power in the scientific world will decide. And once government comes into the hands of the scientist, then everything is possible.

I have called science, *objective religion*; and religion, *subjective science*.

Once it comes into the hands of science, the world map will be different, because what is the fight between the Russian scientist and the American scientist? They are both working on the same projects; it will be far quicker if they work together. It is sheer stupidity that all over the world the same experiments are being repeated in every nation; it is unbelievable. All these people together can do miracles. Divided, it becomes more expensive.

> **"The future belongs to the scientist, not to the politician. That means we will have to change the word democracy. I have a word for it: meritocracy."**

For example, if Albert Einstein had not escaped from Germany, then who would have won the Second World War? Do you think America and Britain and Russia would have won the Second World War? No. A single man's escape from Germany, Albert Einstein escaping from Germany, has shaped history. All these bogus names: Roosevelt, Churchill, Stalin, Hitler, they don't mean anything. That man did the whole thing because he created the atom bomb. He wrote a letter to Roosevelt: "The atom bomb is ready with me, and unless you use it there is no way to stop the war." He regretted it his whole life, but that's another story. The atom bomb was used, and the moment it was used there was no question of Japan going on fighting. The war was won: Hiroshima and Nagasaki burning ended the Second World War. Albert Einstein was working on the same project in Germany. He could have written to just a different address – instead of to Roosevelt, to Adolf Hitler – and the whole history would have been different, totally different.

The future is going to be in the hands of the scientist. It is not far away. Now there are nuclear weapons, politicians cannot manage to be on top. They know nothing about it, not even the *abc*.

It was said while Einstein was alive that only twelve persons in the whole world understood his theory of relativity. One of those twelve people was Bertrand Russell who wrote a small book for those who could not understand it: *The ABC of Relativity*. He thought that at least they could understand the *abc* – but even that is not possible, because if you can understand the *abc*, then the whole alphabet becomes simple. It is not a question of only understanding *abc*; then *xyz* is not far away. The real problem is to understand the *abc*. Now all these politicians don't understand anything at all. Sooner or later the world is going to be in the hands of the people who have merit.

First it will move into the hands of the scientists. This you can take almost as a prediction that the world is going to move into the hands of the scientists. And then a new dimension opens up. Sooner or later the scientist is going to invite the sage, the saint, because he cannot manage it alone. The scientist cannot manage himself. He can manage everything, but he cannot manage himself. Albert Einstein may know all about the stars of the universe but he knows nothing about his own center.

This is going to be the future: from politicians to scientists, from scientists to religious people – but that will be a totally different kind of world. Religious people cannot go asking for votes. You will have to ask them. You will have to request them. And if they feel that your request is sincere and the need is there, they may act in the world. But remember, it will not be politics at all.

So let me repeat, the politician can become religious if he drops politics; otherwise it is impossible. The religious man can become part of politics, if politics changes its whole character; otherwise it is impossible for a religious man to be in politics. He cannot be a politician.

But the way things are moving, it is absolutely certain that first the world will go into the hands of the scientist, and then from the scientist it will go to the mystics. And only in the hands of the mystics can you yourself be safe.

The world can be really a paradise. In fact, there is no other paradise unless we make one here.

I have always thought that you were against politicians, so I was very much surprised to know that you have blessed Indira Gandhi. Would you like to say something about it?

I am against the political mind. The political mind means the cunning mind; the political mind means the murderous, violent mind. The political mind means the mind that is only interested in dominating others, that is only interested in being in such a position where millions of people's lives are in his hands, this way or that. The politician's mind is the mind of the perfect egoist.

I am certainly against the political mind. I would like a world which does not go round and round the political mind. I would like a world which has the religious quality, not the political quality. At least I would like the political quality of the mind to recede back into the background.

At the center should be the creative mind; politics is destructive. But this cannot happen right now. For millions of years, politics has been in the center, so this cannot happen right now. A great meditative energy has to be released first.

> "I am against the political mind, but I know that this cannot happen right now. It may take thousands of years. The beginning has to happen right now, the seed has to be sown right now, but the fruits will come only later on. "

If millions of people become meditators, then slowly, slowly the structure of the energy on this earth will change – will start moving from the political mind to the religious mind. I am against the political mind, but I know that this cannot happen right now. It may take thousands of years. The beginning has to happen right now, the seed has to be sown right now, but the fruits will come only later on. You can become a nonpolitical person right now, and your life will have the flowering. But as far as the whole earth is concerned, it is going to take time. What are we going to do meanwhile?

I have blessed Indira Gandhi because to me she seems to be the least political among the Indian politicians. It will again look strange to you because whatsoever has been said about her, spread about her, rumored about her, is just the opposite. But my own observation is this, that she has the least political mind.

And why do I say so? – these are the reasons. First, had she really been a politician and only a politician she wouldn't have tried to do anything that goes against the Indian tradition. The politician never goes against the tradition. He always follows his own followers. That's a mutual arrangement. Particularly in a democratic system, the politician cannot afford to go against the traditions, because after five years the elections will be there. If you go against people's traditions – right or wrong, that is not the point – if you go against their traditions, they will take revenge.

So real politicians only talk about change, but they never try to change anything. They only talk. The talk is okay, it hurts nobody. Even the masses enjoy the talk. Talk about revolution, but don't try to do it because when you try to do it, many of the traditions and superstitions of the masses will have to be destroyed. And then those people will be angry and in a democratic set-up their anger can be dangerous.

Indira Gandhi tried to do something, sincerely tried to do something. In fact that's what created trouble for her. She was trying to help the poor against the rich. She angered the rich, the people who are powerful; she angered the vested interest. No politician will afford it, no politician can afford it. Talking about great things is allowed. Nobody is worried what you talk about – just don't try to do anything. Go on creating beautiful ideas, but never practice them.

She annoyed the rich people of this country because she was doing something for the poor, and she annoyed the poor because whatsoever she did went against their traditions. For example, she imposed birth control. The Indian masses cannot tolerate it. For thousands of years they have thought that it is God who gives children, and who are you to prevent it? It is a gift from God, that has been their idea. Now the gift is becoming very dangerous. The gift is becoming so dangerous that it is almost suicidal. No politician would have tried that. Let the country go to its death – who bothers?

Since Morarji Desai came into power, all the programs for birth control have been put aside. And that is the only hope for this country. If this country can survive, the only hope is to reduce your population. Already there are too many people. Seventy-five percent of the people are living below human standards. Fifty percent of the people are almost starving. Within twenty-five years, by the end of this century, the whole country will be starving. But that is not the point.

The politician thinks only of his power now. He will be here as prime minister for five or ten years at the most. Who cares what happens later on? Why should he risk his power and position? Indira risked it. Hence I call her the least political person in Indian politics.

Secondly, she started succeeding in her programs. That is dangerous; you shouldn't succeed. If the man in power fails, all other politicians are happy. Because the man in power is failing – that is their chance. If the man in power succeeds, there is no chance for them ever to come into power. And she was the first Indian prime minister who was succeeding in bringing a certain order in the country, in creating some discipline out of chaos. She was succeeding in raising people's standard of life. She was succeeding in helping people to be more productive and less destructive. She was succeeding in many, many ways.

> "The politician thinks only of his power now. Who cares what happens later on?"

But that angers other politicians. Now what is their chance? Other politicians live only on the failure of those who are in power. One shouldn't be successful. There is nothing more dangerous than to succeed.

This is strange, but this is a fact in the history of man. If somebody succeeds, his own success is going to boomerang on him. If she had failed, there would have been no trouble. Then the politicians who were against her would have remained divided, and if they were divided there was no danger for her. But she started succeeding, and their chances to come into power started becoming less and less. They all joined together; they had to join. It was a question of life and death for them – now no question of ideologies.

A strange phenomenon has happened in India, very strange. Morarji Desai is a follower of Mahatma Gandhi, and is in power through the help of those who had murdered Mahatma Gandhi. Strange bedfellows! But when it is a question of life and death, who cares about ideologies? Ideologies are good as playthings, toys. All the Indian politicians of different attitudes, approaches, diametrically opposite ideologies, gathered together, became one force against Indira Gandhi. Why? How did it happen? She was succeeding.

Politicians only pretend; they never really do anything. But she was sincere; she really tried to do something for this country. That's why this country can never forgive her.

Thirdly, Indian bureaucracy is the worst in the world. No work ever happens. Files just go on moving from one table to another table for years and years.

I knew a man who fought a single case in the courts his whole life – for almost fifty years. All the judges died. Whosoever tried his case died: all the lawyers for and against. And finally he himself died, but the case was unfinished. Not only the judges and lawyers died, even the government changed. In 1947 India became independent. The case was started by the British government. Even the government died, another government came into power but the case continued.

If you want to do something in this country, it is impossible with such a bureaucracy. You have to force this bureaucracy to do things. The bureaucracy was angry. It was really the bureaucracy who deceived Indira Gandhi. She was given false reports. She was given false reports that her position was perfectly okay, she could allow an election, she was going to win. She depended on the reports of the bureaucracy. Those reports were false. The bureaucracy was absolutely against her. Nobody has ever forced them to do anything, and she was forcing them to do things.

Since Morarji came, the bureaucracy is perfectly happy. Again things are moving at such a slow pace that nothing ever moves. Morarji himself is a bureaucrat; he started his life as a deputy collector. He knows how the bureaucracy functions; he does not interfere. If you are just there to be in power – that is the mind of a politician – you don't interfere. You don't make so many enemies.

The rich people were against Indira because she tried to bring the poor people a little higher from their mire. The poor people were angry because she imposed birth control on them forcibly, and it can be imposed only forcibly – otherwise it is not possible. The bureaucracy was against her because she forced the bureaucracy to do things, to implement things, and fast. The whole country was angry. Had she been a politician, this wouldn't have happened.

Fourth, she imposed an Emergency. She was straightforward. Had she been a politician she would have done everything that is done through an Emergency, without imposing the Emergency. That's what is being done now. Everything is being done just as it was done in the Emergency, but without declaring it. The cunning politician always works indirectly, not directly. He is not straightforward.

Morarji Desai said in one of his interviews to the BBC... It was asked by the BBC men, it was particularly deliberately asked for you and the work that is happening here, "Will you allow us freedom to make films in your country?" He said, "I will allow it, unless it is dangerous to our defense."

Now, how are my sannyasins dangerous to the defense of this country? Doing Dynamic and Kundalini and dancing and singing, how can they be dangerous? And if there is something that Morarji thinks is dangerous he can simply tell the BBC people and all the other TV agencies that have asked to film the ashram, "Make your film, but your film will have to go through the censor board." So simple! If you feel that something is going to be against your country, you can cut it. But this is a cunning political mind. Talk about freedom, just talk about freedom, that's all – and go on creating more and more bondage for people.

Indira was straightforward, she declared the Emergency. She

was honest. The Emergency was needed. This country can only be changed if things are to be taken very seriously, as if the country is at war. Unless things are taken in that proportion and that intensity, as if the country is at war, nothing is going to happen. And the war is there.

The war is with the population explosion. It is far more dangerous than to be in a war with Pakistan or China because China cannot destroy you, neither can Pakistan destroy you. Maybe China can take a few miles of land, but the population explosion is the real enemy. The children that are going to come will destroy you. Things are in a dangerous situation. It is the greatest crisis that India has ever faced in the past; it knows no way to tackle it. Things have to be taken seriously.

That was the effort behind imposing the Emergency. But imposing an Emergency in a democratic country is dangerous. It can be done only by a nonpolitical mind. It can be done only by one who really wants to change the situation, whatsoever the cost. She risked her power, her prime ministership, to change the course of the history of this country.

This Emergency angered the journalists and other media people. And no politician ever likes to anger the journalists because much depends, too much depends on them. It can be safely said that fifty percent of Indira's fall was made possible by the Indian journalists. They were getting angry and angrier. They weren't allowed to gossip, they weren't allowed to make rumors, they weren't allowed what they call "freedom of the press." So when the Emergency was removed, they took great revenge. It is how the human mind functions. A politician would have been alert about it.

Fifth, her son, Sanjay Gandhi, entered politics. A real politician, a cunning politician, would have allowed him to enter only from the back door; otherwise, others become jealous. She allowed him to enter from the front door, and the whole country became jealous.

There is no reason to prevent anybody from entering politics. Even though the person happens to be the son of the prime minister, he has every right to enter politics like anybody else. And Sanjay Gandhi has a certain potential. There was nothing wrong in it, but to allow him through the front door is a nonpolitical thing. She functioned more as a mother and a human being than as a cunning politician.

Her own father never allowed her from the front door; he was more cautious. Again and again, he was asked, "Who after you?" He never mentioned Indira Gandhi – never. Once to a friend he mentioned, "I cannot tell you the name of the person who will succeed me because if I tell you the name then there is no possibility for the poor person to succeed me. Just by mentioning it I will anger all the other people who are competitors, and they will join together against him." There is every possibility he meant "her" not "him." He was a more seasoned politician than Indira Gandhi; he knew the ways of politics.

Indira Gandhi herself came from the back door. But she is more a mother than a politician; she allowed Sanjay Gandhi to enter from the front door. That was dangerous; that became one of the most important causes of her fall. And it was more dangerous because Sanjay has the potential. Sooner or later, he is going to become a prime minister. He has the potential and the guts. It cannot be prevented. But Indira was functioning very nonpolitically.

Morarji Desai is more cunning. His son is also there, but always behind a screen. And those who are even more interested in power go even further. The chief minister of Haryana, Devi Dayal, has disowned his son and saved his seat – saved his power and disowned his son. This is how a politician functions.

Indira Gandhi risked her power and tried to save her son. That is not the way of a politician – maybe the way of a mother, of a human being.

Sixth, the greatest error that a politician can commit, a very fundamental error and very obvious – Indira Gandhi forced all the political parties into jail together. That is so absurd! Even a man like me, who has nothing to do with politics, can see that it is absolutely absurd. If you put all the enemies into jail together, you are forcing them to be united against you.

She should have studied Machiavelli a little more. It is so simple; a politician would never do that. Keep at least half the enemies out of prison, and half the enemies in prison. Keep them fighting, keep them separate, because that is the only way to rule – to divide. This is utterly stupid – putting all your enemies together in jail you have almost imposed unity on them; they cannot avoid it. Now you are the enemy of all of them.

They became friendly, and they saw the point that if they can become friendly and if they can come together, then Indira is gone. This they had not seen for thirty years; for thirty years they had remained divided. Suddenly Indira brought them together, and they became aware that "It is so simple. If we join together then Indira is gone." The Congress Party had ruled for thirty years because the enemies were divided. Indira functioned as a non-politician.

And seventh, after the Emergency, immediately after the Emergency, and after a great effort to impose birth control on the people – when rich people, poor people, the journalists and everybody was annoyed and angry – immediately after the Emergency declaring a general election, again that is incomprehensible.

If she had asked me, I would have told her, "Wait at least for one year. Remove the Emergency, wait for one year." That one year would have done it. The journalist's steam would have been released. People would have forgotten the imposition. People's memories are very short. And in one year the enemies, all the political enemies, would have again fallen into their old habits, and would have started quarreling with each other again.

Immediately giving a general election to the country was utterly unpolitical. That's how she got defeated.

Because of these errors, I say she is the least political of all the Indian politicians, hence I have blessed her. I have blessed her, and I bless her again.

CHAPTER 6

A Divided Humanity

In an interview with Der Spiegel, you made a statement about Hitler, saying you love the man because he's crazy, and also that he lived a life of discipline just as a saint lives in a monastery. You also compared him with Mahatma Gandhi and called him as moral as Mahatma Gandhi. This has caused a great deal of concern and confusion in Germany, Holland, and other European countries. My question is: Is this an accurate reflection of your feelings about Hitler?

It is very easy to misunderstand me.

I did compare Adolf Hitler with Mahatma Gandhi. Obviously, it is difficult to understand because they seem to be totally opposite to each other; but that opposition is only seemingly so. Adolf Hitler created the greatest violence in the world up to now. He killed one million Jews in gas chambers, in concentration camps, and for five years continuously invaded countries, butchered people – children, old men, women, who had nothing to do with the military. They were simple citizens. To compare Adolf Hitler with Mahatma Gandhi seems to be absurd, but it is not.

Mahatma Gandhi preached nonviolence, but Mahatma Gandhi was not a nonviolent man. Preaching is one thing, to live it is totally different. I will give you a few examples which can show you what I mean.

Gandhi used to have an ashram in South Africa, called Phoenix. His wife was continuously tortured by him for the simple reason that she was not willing to clean the toilets of other people of the ashram.

In India it is accepted that only a certain caste – the lowest, the untouchables – do that work. The higher caste people never do that kind of work. Kasturba, Gandhi's wife, was a simple, traditional woman. It was hard for her. Because she refused – she was pregnant – in the middle of the night Gandhi threw her out of the house and told her that unless she feels that she has committed a sin, he will not allow her in the house. A cold night, a pregnant woman in a country where she does not know any language to communicate with people – do you think of this act as nonviolence? I cannot see it as nonviolent. It is pure violence. In the first place, if Gandhi feels it right to clean toilets, he can do it. But to force it on the wife is trespassing on the freedom of the individual – which also is violence.

Gandhi had five sons. The eldest, Haridas, escaped from home because Gandhi would not allow him to go to school. Gandhi was against modern education; he thought modern education – particularly science – had destroyed people's religion, innocence, faith, so he was not going to educate his children. Haridas was very interested in knowing more and more things. Naturally he wanted to be educated; and I don't see that he was wrong. In fact, whatever Gandhi knew was through education, and Gandhi was educated in England. If British education could not destroy him, could not destroy his religiousness, why should he be afraid that his son would be destroyed? But he was so much against it that it came to a climax point. He told Haridas, "Either you stop asking to be educated, or just get lost. Then this is not your home."

> *"Violence is not only killing people. Violence is an attitude, an approach."*

Haridas must have been a courageous child: he left home.

Do you think of this as nonviolence? Violence is not only killing people. Violence is an attitude, an approach. Gandhi was trying to impose his ideology on his son. This is not nonviolence at all. And to tell the small child either to accept his ideology or leave the house and never come back again – this seems to be hard, harsh, ugly.

Haridas left the house and stayed with one of his distant relatives who could understand that his demand was not wrong. He educated him. And because Haridas became educated, Gandhi wouldn't accept him in the house; not only that, he disinherited Haridas and told him he was no longer his son. This is an extremely violent, revengeful attitude.

And in fact, Haridas proved that Gandhi was wrong. He became educated; no religion was lost, no innocence was lost, no faith was lost. If Gandhi was really a nonviolent person, he should have apologized to Haridas and welcomed him home, because he had existentially proved that Gandhi was wrong. But, on the contrary, he was so resentful, so revengeful that he disinherited him.

Gandhi used to say that Hinduism, Mohammedanism, and Christianity are all the same. All the religions of the world teach the same doctrine, the same God. Their languages may be different, but their essentials are not different. Anyone reading Mahatma Gandhi will think him a great synthesizer of all the religions, but that is not true. It was not a philosophical understanding but a political strategy.

In India the majority religion is Hindu, the second major religion is Mohammedan, the third is Christianity. Gandhi wanted these three religions to follow his fight against the British rule. And it was possible only if all three were not religiously antagonistic to each other. So it was a political strategy, and Haridas proved it perfectly. When he was abandoned by Gandhi, disinherited, Haridas became converted to Mohammedanism. The word *haridas* means "servant of God." He told the Mohammedan priest who was converting him, "Please keep my name – of course in the Arabic translation, but with the same meaning." So the name given to him was Abdullah Gandhi. "Abdullah" means the same as Haridas – "servant of God."

Gandhi was furious. Now, in the first place, you have disinherited him, he is no longer your son – why should you be furious? And it is everybody's freedom to choose any path. This is absolutely violent. He said to his wife, "I am not going to see his face again in my life. And remember..." The custom in India is that when the father dies, the eldest son sets fire to his funeral pyre. So Gandhi made it clear to all his sons, wife, friends, followers, that in no case should Haridas be allowed to start the fire at the funeral. He even managed to dominate after death! Certainly his mind must have been really full of hate.

It happened only once....

Where I used to live in Jabalpur, there is a junction railway station, Katni, a hundred miles away, where – just by chance – Gandhi was traveling in one train and Haridas was traveling in another train from another direction. Both trains had to wait at Katni for a train from a third direction to arrive.

Haridas, seeing that his father and his mother were in the train, rushed just to have a look at the old man – he was never revengeful – and to see his mother. As Haridas came close, Gandhi closed the door, closed the windows, and told Kasturba, Haridas' mother – who was really crying because she wanted to see Haridas, just to see him! – told her, "If you want to see him, then go with him. Just as I have abandoned him, you are also abandoned." Haridas is standing outside the compartment – windows closed, door closed – Kasturba is crying, and Gandhi will not allow her even to see her son's face.

Do you think this is nonviolence, compassion, love?

Gandhi had said to an American journalist, Louis Fisher... because Fisher had asked him, "You are against violence. If India becomes independent, what will happen to the biggest army in the world?" – which was in India. "What will happen to your air force, your navy, and all your war weapons?" A relevant question.

Gandhi said, "I will dissolve all armies, send them to the farms to work there, and I will drown all the weapons in the ocean. My country is going to be absolutely nonviolent." India became independent. The army was not dissolved; the question was not even raised. On the contrary, India and Pakistan started a war. The three war planes – the first to go over the Pakistan borders to bomb citizens – were blessed by Gandhi. This is a strange kind of nonviolence.

When India was under British rule, nonviolence was a good policy because India could not have managed any armed revolution against the British – that was impossible. The only way was what Gandhi did: "Fill the prisons. Go and declare to the prison authorities, 'We are for independence. If you want to imprison us, imprison us.'" Now, India is a vast country. Today its population is eight hundred million. Where can you find so many prisons? And Gandhi insisted that no freedom fighter do anything which could provoke and give an excuse to the British government to be violent. "Don't throw a stone at a police station. Don't burn a train, don't dynamite a bridge, because anything done by you will be enough excuse for the British government to kill thousands of people. And we will not be able to stand before the world to say that we are nonviolent, and nonviolent people are being killed who have not done any harm. Then we will not be able to gain the sympathy of the whole world."

This is simple strategy, and Gandhi succeeded in his strategy; he really confused the British government. What to do with this man? He would not do any violence, nor would he allow his followers to do any violence, and if people are not doing anything, how can you start shooting them? On what grounds?

Finally Britain decided to leave India – not because of Gandhi's movement; his movement happened in 1942, and the British government left India in 1947. Revolution brings immediate effect. Cause and effect are joined, not five years apart. The revolution that happened in 1942 in India was crushed within nine days. Never in history has there been such an impotent revolution, ever. Nine days, and the whole revolution had disappeared.

There was no reason for the British government to be afraid of such a revolution and let India be free. India was almost half the empire of Britain. The reason they left was totally different. The reason was that they had exploited India enough; now there was no more possibility to exploit it. On the contrary, it was becoming an economic burden on Britain. They were the rulers, obviously they were responsible for the people, and the responsibility was growing every day as India's population was growing. It is simple arithmetic that if an empire becomes an economic burden on you, then the best way out is to make it free. Let them have their own responsibility. And moreover, it was beautiful to give India freedom while there was no revolution, so you could keep a friendship with the country. You have not been thrown out, but by your own will you have made the country free. You have obliged the country.

> "It is simple arithmetic that if an empire becomes an economic burden on you, then the best way out is to make it free. Let them have their own responsibility."

So as far as Gandhi's nonviolence goes, the moment Britain left India, nonviolence also disappeared. And a strange coincidence is that Gandhi had been for forty years continuously forcing people not to be violent. He had no discipline, no method of meditation that could recreate a man's energy, could transform his being and make him nonviolent. He had only this ideology: "Don't be violent."

And violence is within you. It is man's inheritance of millions of years, it needs tremendous work to change it. Gandhi had not given any idea how it had to be changed. But "Don't be violent" meant repress it, go on repressing. For forty years he managed to force Indians to repress their violence. And his logic was appealing: "If you are violent, Britain is never going to leave India. If you are nonviolent, then sooner or later they will be ashamed of keeping an innocent, nonviolent country in slavery."

So people remained nonviolent for forty years, and as Britain left India, a tremendous violence exploded in India. And the coincidence is, just one million people were killed in that violence; riots between Hindus and Mohammedans killed one million people – exactly the same number as Adolf Hitler killed in Germany! Of course, they arrived from different directions, but both came to the same conclusion.

Who is responsible for the one million people killed in India after independence? Gandhi has to accept that he was responsible for forty years' repression, and when the pressure was gone – Britain had moved with her armies out of the country – it erupted like a volcano.

In fact, Adolf Hitler's violence with the Jews was far more peaceful because he killed people in the most up-to-date gas chambers, where you don't take much time. Thousands of people can be put in a gas chamber, and just a switch is pressed. Within a second you will not know when you were alive and when you died. Within a second, you evaporate. The chimneys of the factory start taking you, the smoke – you can call it the holy smoke – and this seems to be a direct way toward God. The smoke simply goes upward.

But the violence that happened in India was really cruel, ugly, barbarous. Children were mutilated, killed; old men were mutilated, killed. Trains were burned, buses were burned, houses were burned. All over India there was freedom to kill. There was no rule, no government; nobody could prevent it.

But psychologists have not looked into why it happened, who is responsible for it. I make Mahatma Gandhi responsible for it. That's why I had compared Mahatma Gandhi with Adolf Hitler. If you look just at the sentences where I compare them, you may be confused. But if you go into all the details of why I did it, you will not be surprised.

I had compared Adolf Hitler also with so-called saints living in the monasteries. That was not to praise Adolf Hitler – but you know the German mind, they could not get the point. They have never been able to get the point. It was said to condemn the saints in the monasteries. Adolf Hitler really lived like a monk. He used to get up very early in the morning, the way

> *"Neither vegetarianism, nor a structured life, nor celibacy, bachelorhood, is going to transform you."*

monks are supposed to get up. He used to go early to bed, at exactly the time that every monastery follows. He was a vegetarian. To be a vegetarian in India is simple, everybody is, but to be vegetarian in Germany… He never ate any meat, any fish, he was absolutely a vegetarian. He lived his life almost entirely in an underground cell. Just the way monks live in their cells in the monastery, he lived in an underground cell. He was a bachelor almost his whole life, except for the last three hours when he got married.

Hitler never allowed any woman to sleep in his room. His reasons were different: the monks are afraid that they may get interested in the woman; Hitler was also afraid, but his fear was different. His fear was that the woman might kill him when he was asleep. Who knows if she is a spy? He never allowed anybody – man or woman. He would lock the door from the inside, because in sleep anything can be done to you.

He never trusted anybody, he had no friends. He lived a very structured life. That's why I said he lived like a saint in the monasteries. Why do you praise the saints in the monasteries? – because of their disciplined, structured life, ascetic life. But Adolf Hitler fulfills all these conditions.

He never tasted wine. On that point he scores better than your saints, particularly the Christian saints. They are not prohibited from drinking wine. In fact, you may be surprised that the best wineries were Christian monasteries. The best wine has come out of the monasteries. The monks were not only drinking, but making alcohol too. Great religious job!

I was condemning the monks when I compared them with Adolf Hitler. I was condemning Mahatma Gandhi when I compared him with Adolf Hitler. I was not praising Adolf Hitler. I was using him as a comparison. The reasons that you respect a saint – he fulfills them perfectly. The reasons Mahatma Gandhi is thought to be a great soul – Adolf Hitler fulfills perfectly. And yet the man turned out to be the biggest monster in the whole history of humanity.

You can now see my standpoint. Neither vegetarianism, nor a structured life, nor celibacy, bachelorhood, is going to transform you. These things could not transform Adolf Hitler. How could these things transform Mahatma Gandhi? How could these things transform the thousands of saints and monks living in the monasteries? These things have no relevance as far as the transformation of man is concerned.

The Christian saints have been responsible for immense violence throughout two thousand years of Christian history. They have killed Jews, they have killed Mohammedans. They have burned people alive – particularly they have burned millions of women alive. And if Adolf Hitler burned one million Jews in a very scientific, peaceful way – nobody was tortured – what is the difference between these people?

Gandhi managed to repress violence – which was bound to explode one day, and it did explode. And in that explosion he himself was assassinated. Strange, a man who has been teaching nonviolence his whole life is assassinated.

Not much difference... Hitler committed suicide, Gandhi was assassinated, but both died in an unnatural way.

In fact, before Gandhi was assassinated, in his diary, he mentions many times, "Now I would like God to take me away from life." When he was young he had written in his autobiography, "I would like to live one hundred and twenty-five years." And he repeated it again and again until India became independent. When India became independent, his followers...they were not really his followers, because none of them was listening to what he was saying.

He was against smoking, but almost all his political followers, the leaders, were smokers; they were all drinkers. His successor, Pandit Jawaharlal Nehru, was a meat eater; Indira too, was a meat eater. Strange, a country of nonviolent people, a country of vegetarians has been for the last forty years almost continuously ruled by a single family who are not vegetarians. Now again, Indira's son is there on the throne, and he is not a vegetarian either. So those disciples were not listening to him, but they still kept him high in the sky because he had immense influence over the Indian masses. The Indian masses were not interested in his politics, they were interested in his mahatmahood, his saintliness.

> "Prayer is faith, belief in God. You start with a lie!"

His followers were not interested in his mahatmahood. They all laughed behind his back, they thought that he was a crackpot. But they were interested in political power, and that man had the whole country in his hands. So until these political leaders came into power, they went on listening to Gandhi. The moment they were in power, nobody bothered about Gandhi.

Gandhi said, "I have become absolutely useless. Nobody listens to me, nobody is ready to follow my advice. It would be good if God took me away from life. Now I do not want to live for one hundred and twenty-five years."

Asking God to release you from your body is a religious way of being suicidal. He could not commit suicide, because that would go against his whole philosophy. But he was waiting for somebody else to do the dirty job. And one man, Nathuram Godse, did it.

The last words of Gandhi when he was assassinated were, "Ah, God!" My feeling is that he felt immensely relieved. He was in a constant torture after the freedom. First the explosion of violence all over the country – one million people dead, many more crippled, blinded, their hands cut off, their legs cut off; many more made beggars because their houses were burned.... And this man was thinking that after independence there would be an era of nonviolence, peace. His intentions were good, but his understanding was poor. His intentions were good, but how to implement those intentions in reality, he was absolutely unaware.

He was not a meditator. He used to pray every day, but prayer is not meditation. Prayer is faith, belief in God. You start with a lie! You don't know whether God exists or not; or even if he exists, whether he bothers about prayers or not. Gandhi's religion is just the religion of the mediocre masses, it is not the religion of an enlightened man. So he was praying every day, his followers were praying every day, and all their prayers resulted in a chaos.

That was the answer from God. Forty years of prayer, discipline, celibacy... And about small things, Gandhi was really nasty. He wouldn't allow anybody to drink tea. In his ashram, tea was prohibited, coffee was impossible to bring in. The question of alcohol did not arise. For forty years the people followed all kinds of ascetic disciplines, prayed morning and evening – and the answer was millions of people either murdered or half-murdered, and Gandhi himself assassinated. If this is the result of practicing nonviolence, then I don't think there is any difference practicing violence.

Adolf Hitler and Mahatma Gandhi both ended the same way. They both landed their countries in the same mess.

I have said I have a certain love for Adolf Hitler, for the simple reason that at least he was straightforward; Gandhi was not. Adolf Hitler was not cunning. Whatever he wanted to do, he did. He was a little crazy, but a crazy man managed to be the world's greatest conqueror. He had some integrity, some insight. Germany is a small country, but he managed to threaten the whole world. And he was not a hypocrite. That's why I have said I love the man.

I cannot love Mahatma Gandhi; he was a hypocrite, he was a cunning politician. Adolf Hitler was simply what he was, with no mask. Mahatma Gandhi had a mask, and I hate people who have masks because they are deceiving everybody, including themselves.

When you have a mask, slowly, slowly as many people start believing in your mask, you also start believing in your mask. And obviously, if you stand with a mask before a mirror, the mirror can only show your mask, not your real face. Adolf Hitler had no mask. Mahatma Gandhi had a very thick mask.

In the history books, Adolf Hitler will be condemned, Mahatma Gandhi will be praised. But I want it to be on record that Adolf Hitler was more sincere a man than Mahatma Gandhi.

Mahatma Gandhi used to say, "I love all of my disciples equally." Each year there was an election of the Indian national congress, of which he was the uncrowned king, and whomsoever he wanted to be the president was chosen. But one man, Subhash Chandra Bose, who was not a believer in nonviolence although he was a member of the Indian national congress, stood for the presidency in 1939. I was very small, but that is the only convention that I have attended – because it was very close to my home. It was just thirteen miles from Jabalpur, where Subhash Chandra presided over the congress. Without Gandhi's blessings, without even asking him, he stood for that position. Gandhi was very angry. His followers suggested that Jawaharlal Nehru could be put to oppose him, but Gandhi had really a political mind – perhaps better than Machiavelli. He said, "That is not a good idea. Jawaharlal is my most precious disciple. If

he wins, nothing is gained; people will say he had Gandhi's blessings. But Subhash has also the same charismatic personality, perhaps more charismatic than Jawaharlal, and there is every possibility
that Subhash may win. Then it will be a double defeat: the man who
has my blessings is defeated, and Jawaharlal's whole future will be
dark. That defeat will put him into the back row."

So Gandhi managed to persuade a man who was not known in
the country at all, was not of the caliber of Subhash Chandra or
Jawaharlal – Pattabhi Sitaramayya. Nobody had even heard his
name. The strategy was that with Gandhi's blessings, even a person
who was not known in the country at all could win the election. "If
he wins, then that will be a great victory. If he loses, we can say that
it was clear that he would lose, because Subhash is a world-famous
name, and Pattabhi Sitaramayya is not even a provincial name." And
Gandhi forgot all about the fact that he loves his disciples equally.

Of course, Subhash was victorious, even with the declaration of
Gandhi that "Pattabhi Sitaramayya's defeat will be my defeat." That
was blackmail, blackmailing the masses, that "If you vote against
Pattabhi Sitaramayya you are voting against me; he is simply my
representative." Still Subhash won the elections, became the president. And Gandhi, after Subhash's big victory, did not even congratulate him.

He repeated again, "Pattabhi Sitaramayya's defeat is my defeat."
And just to avoid being present in the convention, the annual convention of the congress – because Subhash would be the president
there – Gandhi pretended to fall sick in Rajkot so that he need not
go. It was so clear that Subhash resigned from the presidency. He
said, "If this is the way that Mahatma Gandhi behaves – in whom we
all have always had immense trust – if he cannot come to the convention just because somebody is victorious who had not taken his
blessings, then it is not worthwhile. Against him I am not going to
remain the president of the congress." He resigned.

Gandhi's whole life has to be studied – not by historians, but by
psychologists, psychoanalysts, who can figure out this man, his cunningness, strategies, his lies, his political games. In comparison to
this, Adolf Hitler is straightforward.

I am not saying that Adolf Hitlers are needed in the world. I am not saying that Adolf Hitler should be worshipped as a messiah. I am simply saying that we are living in a strange world where a man like Mahatma Gandhi, who has done everything undercover, is worshipped, and Adolf Hitler is condemned because he has done everything in the sunlight.

Both have to be condemned.

And when I said I have some love for Adolf Hitler, I meant I have love for sincerity, integrity, courage, straightforwardness. And these qualities were in that man. He misused them. I condemn the way he used his qualities, but I cannot condemn the qualities themselves. Every individual needs those qualities.

But of course, in Germany they must have misunderstood, because Germany has suffered so much because of Adolf Hitler. The wound is still there. Even the name of Adolf Hitler makes the German mind angry. And when I compared him with the Christian saints in the monasteries, of course they were more offended. But what can I do? He lived like a monk.

He did tremendous harm to humanity, but that is another side of his personality. And for that too – I have looked deeply into Adolf Hitler's life – he alone is not responsible. He wanted to be an artist, but no art school in Germany accepted him. Just the entrance examination, and he failed. He was not a great artist, but his intention was to become an artist, a creator. When he failed in art school, he decided to become an architect; he wanted to make new kinds of buildings, new structures. But no school of architecture accepted him. He was in love with a woman who simply rejected him because he was unemployed, uneducated. And of course you know his picture; nobody can say it is beautiful – particularly with that small mustache. He looks worse than Charlie Chaplin. And if any woman just got rid of him, we cannot blame the woman. But one thing is certain, he was rejected in every possible way by the society. No love was given to him. His father was a very strict disciplinarian, continuously condemning him, continuously letting him down. It was his practice to call in the neighbors, and before the neighbors, condemn Adolf Hitler.

This man, finding, "This world does not accept me in any way,

I am just unworthy," started feeling a deep inferiority complex. It is natural: rejection from all sides will make anybody feel an inferiority complex. And the inferiority complex is the cause of what Adolf Hitler became in his life.

He entered the army – that was the only place where he was acceptable because in the army, whether your face is beautiful or ugly is not considered. Ugly is better; in the army we don't need film actors, we need monsters. And in the army he proved very successful – he won awards. And he found out one thing: that as a killer he could prove his superiority in the world; there was no other way. That's how he entered politics, and that's how he became the chancellor of the country. He used army tactics.

When he made his party for the first time, the National Socialist Party, there were only nineteen members – all unemployed, because Germany was defeated in the First World War, and many army people were retired before the usual age. Hitler was also retired, and he was young. These nineteen people were all army people who had been thrown into unemployment; they made this party. And it is a miracle of history that nineteen men managed to come into power within ten years' time.

Their way of working was strange, one which no political party has ever known. This was their strategy. First, they were only nineteen people. They would go to all the other parties' meetings and disturb them. For that, nineteen people were enough. Those nineteen people would be sitting separately in the crowd, and suddenly they would start beating people.

Naturally, if nineteen people start beating people, others will stand up, others will get involved in saving or beating – but the meeting is finished. And by the time the people reach home, they are all hurt. Somebody has broken his leg, somebody has a fracture, somebody's head is bleeding.

The biggest party in those days was the Communist Party. Slowly it became clear that it was dangerous to go to any Party meeting. So Communist Party leaders would call the meeting, advertise the meeting, put the posters all over the city – and nobody would turn up to listen to the leaders.

Then Adolf Hitler started having his meetings. And on his posters it was written, "Don't be worried – in this meeting there is not going to be any disturbance. And we will see that if anybody does any harm, he is finished." Of course, those nineteen people were standing at the gates. Soon it became clear in Germany that only Adolf Hitler's meetings were safe.

People are political animals. They could not go to other parties, but they would like to know what is going on. They all started gathering at Adolf Hitler's meetings. It was a miracle the way he managed. Thousands and thousands of people would come and spread the news that in Adolf Hitler's meeting there was no problem; nobody was hurt, no chaos, no beating. This is the party! And people started joining it, because this was the only leader they were listening to. Within ten years, Hitler was the head of the government. And then he used all his qualities in a wrong way.

He had tremendous capacity to arouse people's feelings, emotions, and he used it in a very scientific way to influence people. He used to have big rallies. For example, if a rally was happening in Munich, then all his followers from other cities would go there. But the people of Munich would feel that Munich had so many followers of Adolf Hitler! The rallies were arranged in the night with burning torches in everyone's hands. Thousands of people with burning torches in their hands in the dark night left a tremendous mark on people's minds.

When it was in Berlin, then the Munich people and other people would be in Berlin. Slowly, slowly he convinced the whole country that "The whole country is in my hands." It was not true, but the way he worked it out proved perfectly successful.

This man would not have been there if he had been accepted by an art school, or an architecture school, or by a woman. This man would not have been the head of the government. There would not have been a Second World War.

What I want to say to you is: never reject a person. Even if you have to for certain reasons, make it as polite and nice as possible. Rather than making him feel unworthy of you, it is better to let him feel that you are unworthy of him. Then we can stop Adolf Hitlers in the world; otherwise it is impossible, they will be coming.

The parents have to learn that the child should not be insulted, humiliated, condemned. If you want to help him, love him more. Appreciate what is good in him rather than emphasizing what is bad. Talk about his goodness. Let the whole neighborhood know how nice and beautiful a boy he is. You may be able to shift his energy from the bad side to the good side, from the dark side to the lighted side, because you will make him aware that this is the way to get respect, this is the way to be honored.

> "The parents have to learn that the child should not be insulted, humiliated, condemned."

And you will prevent him from doing anything that makes him fall down in people's eyes.

But parents go on doing the same as Adolf Hitler's parents were doing. Teachers go on doing the same. Priests go on doing the same: calling people sinners, condemning them for everything. The natural outcome is that everybody is carrying an inferiority complex. And that is the most dangerous thing to carry within you. It hurts, and one wants to get rid of it. And the only way to get rid of it is to prove to the whole world that you are not inferior. Only when the whole world accepts that you are not inferior, will you be able to feel that the inferiority complex was wrong.

The inferiority complex leads people into politics, makes people presidents, prime ministers. The inferiority complex leads people into all kinds of ambitions, crimes. Unless humanity is completely freed from this complex, we cannot have a peaceful world. And we need it very urgently, because if we cannot manage to have people who are contented with themselves, happy with themselves, relaxed with themselves – with no grudge, no complaint against the world – then the third world war is just on the horizon. Any stupid politician, to prove himself the biggest one, the one who started the third world war, is going to do it.

The trouble is increasing. If nuclear weapons were only confined to the hands of America and the Soviet Union, there would not be much danger because both powers are equally balanced, and both know that nobody is going to win and everybody is going to be finished. The whole of life will be destroyed. But other countries are trying now to make nuclear weapons – smaller countries which have no place in the world of powerful people, but they have riches. For example, in the Middle East, the oil countries have all the riches that you need to make nuclear weapons. Now who is going to prevent them? They can start a nuclear war. And once it is started it will pull all the nuclear powers into it, because a nuclear weapon can be faced only by another nuclear weapon.

Now poor countries like India are trying to make nuclear weapons. Half the country is dying, without food, and India is exporting wheat to other countries because it needs money for a nuclear plant.

It is becoming more and more urgent that we create people who have no inferiority complex, people who have a certain serenity, silence, people who have a deep contentment within themselves, people who are no longer ambitious. We need a non-ambitious humanity; only then can the cloud of death that is looming on the horizon be avoided.

My people can do it. There is nobody else to whom this great responsibility can be given.

My people have no ambitions. They rejoice without any reason. They dance and sing – they don't need any cause for dancing and singing, dance in itself is cause enough.

> *"Everybody is carrying an inferiority complex. And that is the most dangerous thing to carry within you."*

We have to spread this belt of energy around the earth. This is the only protection for humanity and life on the earth.

All over the world, people are being tortured. At the present time, reports are surfacing every day of unbelievable atrocities committed by man against man. From where does this desire to torture others

arise? Do such perverted acts stem from a deep sense
of frustration and the need to take revenge against
society? Please comment.

Man's whole history is a history of torture, murder, rape. But in
the past it was not possible to know about the whole world, what was
happening; people knew only about local things. Now the earth has
become so small that within minutes, wherever anything happens,
it spreads all over the world. The media has made people aware of
man's reality. In the past it remained hidden. Now it has surfaced.

There are reasons why man is so inhuman. The reasons are
many, but the few most important ones should be understood.

One, all the religions of the world have been teaching unnatural
things to humanity – celibacy, renouncing the pleasures and comforts of life, living in poverty. For centuries they have been telling
these things to people, and they have kept the people uneducated,
illiterate. But an explosion in the contemporary world of education
has created a tremendous problem. Now people know that what has
been told to them was not right – it was not according to nature, it
was against nature. They are full of rage against the whole past. The
religions have corrupted their minds, have led them to perverted
sexual practices. The religions have put
one man against another. There are three
hundred religions on the earth, and each
claims that it is the only ultimate truth, all
others are false.

> "In every way
> science has made
> the whole
> humanity one."

Now, anybody who has a little intelligence can see the point that there can be
only one kind of religiousness, unnamed – just like science. You don't
call it Jewish science, Mohammedan science, Hindu science, Christian
science. Just to call it science is enough; its rules are universal.

Religion is the science of the inner world. Its rules also are universal. But these three hundred religions have been teaching you
just the opposite. They have been teaching you rituals which don't
lead you inside. They have been teaching you about a God who
lives above the clouds; nobody has seen him. They have been

teaching you commandments written three thousand years ago, written five thousand years ago – written, and you have to live according to them.

They have encaged you. In every possible way you are chained – not only your body, but your spirit. Hence, everywhere atrocities are surfacing. They have been surfacing down the ages, but the media to inform you about the reality that is happening all around the earth was missing. Education was missing. Now you are educated – whether you are a Jew or a Christian or a Hindu or a Buddhist, in the same way, in the same science, the same laws.

In every way science has made the whole humanity one. But religions go on carrying the hangover of the past, dividing man against man.

The violence that they have repressed for centuries has come to a climax. The people want to take revenge, because they have been mistreated, they have been deceived by the people they have trusted – by their prophets, their messiahs, their incarnations of God. These people have been the greatest criminals. They divided humanity. They divided you, split you into body and soul: you have to torture your body if you want to know the soul. So for thousands of years people have been torturing their bodies; that was the only way to become saintly. But now it is difficult to convince people that by torturing their bodies they will become holy. There seems to be no sense in it. Man has been divided into man and woman. Half of humanity consists of women, and they have lived a life of slavery, torture, indignity. They are rebelling. Man is rebelling against the past unconsciously. He is enraged by the whole human history. And he is so full of anger, violence, that any small thing brings it up, and it starts spreading like a wildfire.

Secondly, man is tremendously frustrated because the leaders of mankind in the past have been giving him hope, hope of a paradise beyond death. Not a single person has returned after death and given his eyewitness evidence that there is a paradise, that there is a God, that your acts will be judged – you will be thrown into eternal hell or into the eternal blissfulness of paradise.

Nobody has ever returned. Nobody knows anything about life

after death, and people have been sacrificing their present for an unknown future. Now they cannot do it anymore, they have done enough. They want paradise here and now. The leaders cannot supply the goods that they have been promising them. Beyond death, of course, they are ready to give you anything you want, but people want it now. That creates a great hopelessness, frustration, meaninglessness.

> "Man has immense capacity to love. If his love is given freedom, he will never commit anything that goes against love."

People have not been taught the art of living beautifully, the art of being graceful, the art of being silent, meditative. Instead of teaching these authentic realities, which can be done right now, their minds were taken away from the present to some unknown future – nobody knows whether it exists or not. Now, because people have become literate, educated, they can see the great deceit. They have been cheated, and a great anger is there. Not only their life but millions of lives for centuries have been exploited by these cheaters.

Religious priests have been parasites sucking your blood. Now it is absolutely impossible for those religions to exist anymore. They should disappear gracefully, and allow a new way of life which is centered in the present, so that something can be done to human psychology.

Man has immense capacity to love. If his love is given freedom, he will never commit anything that goes against love. Man has immense capacity to be compassionate. He will not commit violence on any slight excuse. But he has to be awakened! The religions have been giving him opium, and for thousands of years they have made him completely unconscious. It was good for them – they could exploit people easily. All the vested interests were together: the politician, the priest, the pedagogue, were all together because if man becomes awake, there is no need for politicians; he will see them as criminals. There is no need for priests; he will see them as the greatest cheats that have existed ever.

The pope goes on quoting Jesus Christ, and for centuries you have listened to, "Blessed are the poor." The rich are cursed because even a camel can pass through the eye of a needle, but the rich man cannot pass through the gates of paradise.

And why are people poor? Every religion has given some explanation, has to give one. The Christians are poor because God is very loving to you. You are the blessed; he is preparing you for paradise. This is a test of your trust. And in Christianity, Mohammedanism, Judaism, there is only one life. So the rich person is born without any past life in which he would have committed some evil acts; that's why God has not given him the test of trust and has taken away the opportunity of entering into paradise.

A strange God! He makes people rich, comfortable, luxurious, because he is against them. But why is he against them? They have not done anything. This is their only life! Why has he chosen a few people to be rich, and many people to be poor? All these explanations are bogus; and the contemporary mind is becoming clear about all these explanations, that they were strategies to keep the poor, poor, and to make the rich richer.

In a country like India no revolution has ever happened, although the whole country is poor. In the hands of only a few families, all the riches of the country have gathered. The whole country is starving, hungry, but they have accepted it patiently up to now.

> **"God is the invention of the vested interests."**

There is a limit to everything. Now they are burning. They know they have been cheated, badly cheated. So there are going to be riots, there are going to be killings. And the responsibility goes to your prophets, your messiahs, your messengers of God – and finally, to God. If God exists anywhere, he is the greatest criminal. To create a world with so much hatred, anger, rage, violence...

This is something strange. You make something wrong, and if it behaves wrongly then you punish it. Who has made you a sexual being? If God wanted celibacy, there was no problem for him. If he can create the whole world within six days, can't he manage that man is born without sex, without greed, without jealousy, without anger, without hate? No, God has made a man full of all these things. And you need not learn anger, hate, jealousy; they are instinctive, they are God-given.

Meditation, you will have to learn – God has not given that to you. This God must be nuts! He has not given you the most precious thing, the art of knowing yourself. In fact, he was against all knowledge. He prevented Adam and Eve from eating from the tree of knowledge and from eating from the tree of eternal life. Can you think of this God as divine, who is preventing his children from wisdom and from the taste of eternal life? These are the two things that he should have insisted on: "First taste these two trees, and then the whole Garden of Eden is yours."

But this God is the invention of the vested interests. The priests never wanted people to be educated, they never wanted the people to become intelligent, because there was danger. In their education, in their intelligence, people will start asking questions. And the priests don't have any authentic answers, because all that the priests have created in the name of religion is fiction – and ugly fiction.

Now the new generation is becoming aware everywhere that this God has to be dropped. Nietzsche said, "God is dead and man is free." But the younger generation wants God not to be dead, they want to murder him. Just an easy death does not appeal; they want to murder him! Man has come of age, he is mature. He can see how he has been deceived, and he has to destroy everything that has deceived him.

But the priests are very cunning; cunningness is their profession. They are professional exploiters, parasites, because for centuries they have done nothing else; they have become very skillful. So rather than allowing you to burn the Bible, to get rid of the Vatican, to kill God, they go on diverting you – Christians against Mohammedans, Mohammedans against Hindus, Hindus against Buddhists You are so full of rage that you have lost all reason, you simply want to destroy. And the priests are using this situation. If they don't use it, you will destroy them! So all over the world religions are fighting, nations are fighting, races are fighting.

Who is creating all this? The people who have dominated you

for centuries know perfectly well that your anger, your hatred has to be diverted; otherwise, they will be the targets.

They are all against me for a single reason – that I want your rage to go in the right direction. I don't want to divert it. I want you to meditate and, in silence, see what has been done to man in the whole of history. And out of your silence and peace, if you feel that something has to be destroyed because it has been hindering the growth of man, his consciousness, that destruction will be totally different. It will not be of people; it will not be directed to other human beings who belong to other groups. It will not be between Americans and Soviet people – they have both been exploited by different kinds of priests.

> *"I want you to meditate and, in silence, see what has been done to man in the whole of history."*

Communism is the latest religion. It has its own priests, it has its own holy *Das Kapital*. It has its own trinity – Marx, Engels, Lenin. It has replaced the old religion. There is no need for Americans to destroy Soviet Russians, or Russians to destroy Americans. If we are intelligent, all the politicians – Soviets and Americans – should be imprisoned immediately. And the masses can do it! They just have to be awakened as to who is the real enemy.

The boundaries of all the countries should be dissolved. They don't exist on the earth, only on the map. The whole humanity is one, and the whole humanity should pool all its energies. We can make this earth a paradise.

We are living comfortably here, we are enjoying everything that is beautiful. We are rejoicing, dancing, singing – you will not see long faces here. And nobody is bothered about God – strange! Nobody is bothered about heaven and hell. Those are stupid questions. Why waste your intelligence on stupid questions?

People are so loving, so compassionate – they just need to be made aware of their great potential. People are intelligent – they just have to be given a chance to sharpen their intelligence. The whole world has been fed with the idea of belief. All the religions want you to believe, have faith. That destroys your intelligence. That's their way of destroying your intelligence, keeping you retarded. In my commune, belief is nonexistent.

We trust in doubt because doubt sharpens intelligence, it creates questions for which you have to find answers. This is the way your intelligence becomes sharp. We teach doubt, we teach skepticism, we teach agnosticism. Agnosticism means, be sincere about one thing – what you know and what you don't know. And if you don't know something, accept that "I don't know." This will be punished in the outside world. The outside world respects hypocrites. Whether you know or not, you have to pretend that you know.

The American Boy Scouts have rejected and expelled a brilliant young man – just fourteen years of age. He was their best cadet; he was always first in everything. Why did he have to be expelled? – for a single reason, because he was an intelligent boy. They were filling in the form for higher promotion, in which it is asked, "Do you believe in God?" He simply said, "I don't know. I don't know God, how can I believe or disbelieve?"

> "We trust in doubt because doubt sharpens intelligence, it creates questions for which you have to find answers."

Do you see how people's intelligence is killed? A boy is being agnostic, and absolutely correct: he says, "I don't know. And without knowing you ask me to believe?" Rather than answering him, they expelled him. Belief in God is absolutely necessary for every Scout. Tricky ways of keeping people retarded!

In the First World War, for the first time, psychologists suggested that when soldiers were recruited their mental age should be checked. And they were all shocked because the average mental age of all their soldiers was only thirteen years! Things have not changed. You may be eighty years old with a thirteen-year-old mind. Naturally you will find anguish, tension, worries. You will find yourself in a very confused situation. Your body is allowed to grow, your mind is stopped. From the very childhood you have to believe in some religion, in some absolutely fictitious ideas, ultimate lies. And once a child starts believing in ultimate lies, his intelligence stops growing.

Here, we don't have a belief system; we don't have any faith in which you have to be indoctrinated. We are allowing our people to be as deeply agnostic as possible. And why fear? If God is there and you inquire, question, you will find him. The fear is that if you doubt and inquire you will not find him. That's why doubt has to be from the very beginning completely erased from your mind.

> "Doubt is the method of science. Scientists are not afraid; they go on doubting and questioning every hypothesis, experimenting."

Doubt is the method of science. Scientists are not afraid; they go on doubting and questioning every hypothesis, experimenting. And only if they come to some conclusion which is supported by evidence, supported by experiments, supported by intelligence, and you cannot doubt it, is it accepted. And then too, it is accepted only hypothetically, because perhaps tomorrow you may have better instruments, better minds, better people, and they may find some loopholes in it. They may find that something else is more accurate, more right.

So in science there is no belief, ever. Doubt brings you to a hypothesis. A hypothesis means, for the time being you believe in it – but only for the time being. If tomorrow somebody goes ahead and declares that we can move on, the old hypothesis is dissolved; then the new hypothesis takes its place until you come to something which is indubitable. But it is a great surprise. The moment you find the indubitable, you don't believe in it, there is no need. It is your own experience.

> "Truth needs no belief. Only lies need beliefs."

Truth needs no belief. Only lies need beliefs.

The whole young generation around the world is certainly at a very angry stage. But we have to make the young people aware…because if your leaders who have exploited you are still your leaders, they will exploit your anger too, they will direct it in wrong directions. And that is what is happening.

In India, my experience was that it was so easy to create a riot. For example, Mohammedans believe that music is something evil, so before their mosque you cannot play music – a flute, or a band. You have to stop playing it, move silently before the mosque, and then you can start again. Even in marriages... In India, the marriage procession is something beautiful to see – music, dance. But if the marriage party comes in front of a mosque and continues its music and dance, immediately there will be a riot. Soon Hindus will be killing Mohammedans, Mohammedans will be killing Hindus.

If you want to start a riot, just hang a dead cow in front of a Hindu temple – the cow may have died by herself, that does not matter – and immediately you have put the whole city on fire. Anybody can do it! Politicians are continuously doing it. Religious leaders are continuously doing it. Whenever they see that the anger is turning toward them, they immediately do some small thing: the anger moves, and people destroy themselves.

The other thing to understand very deeply is that scientists have discovered every animal has a territorial imperative. He has a certain territory; for example, around him for thirty yards nobody should enter. If you remain out of his territory, he will not in any way be upset by you, you can remain there. But the moment you trespass the boundary line, immediately the animal becomes dangerous.

Every animal has a territorial imperative. Man comes from the animals. You all feel once in a while to be left alone. Always in a crowd... What happened to your territory? Why do you feel at ease in your home? Why do you feel beautiful in a vast forest or sitting on the beach seeing the immense ocean? It gives you a vast area around you, which is something very essential. But the world is overcrowded. Wherever you are, you are in a crowd. And the world goes on becoming more and more overcrowded. This overcrowding is one of the psychological reasons why people are so on edge. Any moment, anything, and they are ready to fight – in three thousand years, man has fought five thousand wars.

Everybody is encroached upon; and the pope, the Hindu *shankaracharya*, Ayatollah Khomeini – they all go on preaching against birth control, against abortion, against the pill. They want the world to be so crowded – and it will be so crowded – that there is not going to be any elbow room. There will not be any need to go to any meeting; wherever you are, you will be in a meeting. But these idiots keep saying around the world... India is fifty percent ready to become another Ethiopia. In Ethiopia one thousand people have been dying every day for the whole year. Now it is no longer news at all, nobody bothers. It has been accepted that Ethiopians die, one thousand every day. The same will soon be the case in India. The same will be the case in other third-world countries because they are all growing so fast. And nobody is ready to tell these people that they are teaching simple nonsense.

The pope visits Africa, where the birthrate is the highest in the world. People are utterly poor, and he is teaching them that they should not use any birth control methods; it is against God. But there is not much difference between Ethiopia and America, because in America also people like Reverend Falwell are teaching against abortion, against birth control. And what is the reason? – because God is sending people children and you prevent him. This is against God.

But I cannot understand that God cannot remove a small pill? He managed to part the ocean for Moses and his whole company to pass. He went against the law of nature, he managed to give birth to Jesus Christ without a father. He seems to be a skillful man, he can remove the pill! He can change the nature of the pill so that the woman who takes the pill gives birth to two children instead of none. Naturally, people will stop taking the pill, because this is dangerous; you cannot go against God. If God wants people, he can create them.

There are so many millions of planets around, so many solar systems, but only this earth is evolved to the point of human consciousness, only on this earth have there been a few people who have reached the ultimate in consciousness – enlightenment.

Why destroy this earth? It has enriched the whole of existence, and the rest of existence is empty. God can manage to send people to any other planet, any other place. But no, Reverend Falwell wants God to go on sending more people here. Mother Teresa wants more people here. The pope wants more people here, because these poor people are vulnerable, ready to become Christians, Catholics. These poor people and their children will be on the streets, and Mother Teresa can gather the orphans and make the Catholics.

> "Poor people are needed because the religions cannot convert rich people."

And poor people are needed because the religions cannot convert rich people. The uneducated are needed, the orphans are needed because Christians cannot get hold of the educated people. Their own educated young people are getting out of hand. Their churches are empty, the young generation does not go there anymore. They need to fill their churches, their congregations, and their numbers must come from poor countries. And the poor people cannot argue against what they are saying, that God sends people. It has been accepted for centuries that God sends people.

Nobody knows about God, and if he is omnipotent, all-powerful, then whatever you do – any birth control method, anything, abortion, he is all-powerful – can't he do something so that you cannot prevent him from sending people?

God cannot do anything because he does not exist! These reverends and popes and bishops, these are the people who want the world to become as poor as possible – because the poor man is ready to pray, he is ready to go to the church. The poor man is always ready for paradise, heaven, hell. He has no guts, no intelligence to deny anything. Already he is so much in suffering, how can he deny the existence of paradise? That is his only hope, that after death... It is only a question of a few years more of suffering, and then there is an eternity of pleasures – all the pleasures that religions deny here, renounce here! Strange argument...strange logic.

Mohammedans are not allowed to drink alcoholic beverages here on the earth, but in their heaven there are rivers of wine, champagne, and all kinds of alcoholic beverages which you can choose. Rivers flowing, not bottles – you can drink, you can jump in, you can swim, you can drown, you can do anything! Here, alcohol is a sin. Can't you see the stupidity of the logic? Here it is sin. Those who don't drink will become virtuous, they will enter paradise. And there, these saints will be rewarded with beautiful women who always remain young, who do not perspire, who do not need any deodorant; they are always fresh and always virgin. Their virginity is unspoilable; all the saints can make love to them, they are still virgin.

Your saints who here on the earth renounced the woman, the home, the family and all comforts, and lived in poverty – you reward them with these things? As far as I can see, these saints will be simply shocked when they enter paradise, that other popes are making love under the trees. They will not be able to believe it.

I have heard…

An old saint died. His whole teaching was celibacy. And after a few days one of his chief disciples died. The disciple was very excited that he would be meeting his master again. He inquired about him. People showed him: "You will find him under that tree near the river. Perhaps he may recognize you, or he may not recognize you because he is so drunk. Somehow we have pulled him out of the river."

One thing is good: you cannot die in heaven, there is no death; so you can drown but you will live. There is no way to commit suicide in heaven. "We have just pulled him out. He is lying there under the tree."

The disciple rushed there – he could not believe his eyes. He closed his eyes because his old master, naked, had a beautiful woman in his lap, holding her and playing with her, swaying with her. He could not believe it. But then he thought, "Perhaps this is the reward for my master's great celibacy, renunciation, living in poverty, torture. This must be…" because he had never seen such a beautiful woman.

He just fell down at the feet of the master and said, "Master, you are well rewarded."

Before the master could speak, the woman said, "You idiot, you don't understand anything! He is not being rewarded, I am being punished!"

But the poor people have always hoped for heaven. That hope

keeps them suffering patiently; otherwise, there is no reason for them to suffer. Just a little understanding...

The population has to decrease; and immediately, with the population going down, all these atrocities will stop. People need space. Everybody needs a certain space; that space gives him a certain spiritual freedom. Everybody wants to live comfortably, luxuriously – that is natural. But this small earth cannot support so many people.

Popes, *shankaracharyas*, Reverend Falwells – all these people should be behind bars, sentenced for their whole life. These people are wild animals let loose in the world! They should be first tamed, and if they are tamed they can enter a circus – but not the world again. The world's population has to be one fourth of what it is. Then everybody will have space, everybody will have enough – more than enough; everybody will be satisfied, contented, nourished.

And the world needs only one thing – not great scriptures, just a simple method of becoming silent, of becoming yourself, of coming to your innermost center. That center is the temple, the synagogue, the church. There is no other church, no other synagogue.

> "Everybody wants to live comfortably, luxuriously – that is natural. But this small earth cannot support so many people."

Don't go anywhere. Go inside, inward. And there is your paradise, your wisdom, your eternal life. A man who knows his wisdom and his eternal life cannot behave the way people are behaving all around the world.

Every politician should be forced to participate in a school of meditation, and unless he graduates from there he cannot stand for any political post. All politicians, unless they are meditative, are disqualified. If they have any sense of dignity they should renounce, they should immediately resign from their posts. They don't know themselves, what are they doing there? They don't know themselves and they are controlling millions of people and their lives.

My religion consists only of one word: meditativeness. It has no prayer because there is nobody to whom you can pray. You are here, a reality. Why not go in and find out from where your life comes, the source of your life? The source of your intelligence? The source of your love?

Go deep inside, and you will be surprised that hate, anger, jealousy all exist only on the periphery. In the innermost center of your being there is only love and love and love. And it blossoms the moment you reach there, and spreads all over your periphery.

Just as when you bring light in a dark room, darkness disappears, the moment you bring your silence, your peace, your love to your periphery, all the darkness that consisted of jealousy, violence, hatred, anger, competitiveness, disappears. You have not to do anything about it, you have not to control it: it is not there at all.

You cannot control darkness. Either it is there, or you bring a candle in, or light a candle which is already there. And after the light you never ask, "What to do about the darkness now?" It simply is not found.

> "we are not teaching equality, we are not communists. Communism is outdated. We are teaching meditativeness, and the feeling of equality arises of its own accord."

Humanity has only one saving device available, and that is meditation. Everything else has failed. Give a try to meditation.

Here, people are meditating. There is no competition, no stealing, no hurting anybody. Nobody feels himself higher than the other. And we are not teaching equality, we are not communists. Communism is outdated. We are teaching meditativeness, and the feeling of equality arises of its own accord. You need not have a dictatorship of the proletariat to enforce equality on people. Any enforced thing is not going to last long, because deep down whatever you have repressed is there. And it is gathering more and more energy, it is becoming a cancer. Equality cannot be imposed.

But a loving person does not feel himself superior to anybody or inferior to anybody. These two complexes, the inferiority complex and superiority complex, simply disappear from his being. He is just like a tree or a cloud or a mountain, enjoying his being. And the moment you start enjoying your being, rejoicing in your being, you cannot hurt anybody. It is impossible. You can hurt somebody only if you are yourself hurting, if you are carrying wounds within you. When you are healed and whole, your vision about everybody else simply changes. You cannot condemn, you cannot humiliate anybody. Your love will not allow you to do that.

> "A decision is possible. Politicians gone, nations are gone. Priests gone, there is only one humanity."

Through meditation we have to create communes around the world – we have many already. We have to create them in every country. If we can make these existential experiments available to the whole humanity, there is a hope that we can free them from the long, long bondage of politicians and priests. In the future, if humanity is to exist, then politicians and priests are not to exist. We have to make a clear choice.

On one side is the whole humanity of innocent people, and on the other side is the company of all the criminals and conspirators against humanity: the politicians, the priests.

And the time has come. We have come to an ultimate crisis where a decision is possible. Politicians gone, nations are gone. Priests gone, there is only one humanity. And then every university can become a place not only to teach you geography, which is stupid, history, which is just rubbish, but to teach you something very essential: meditation, love, the art of living, the art of being human.

Each university should become a temple of wisdom; it is not yet. It is called a university but it is not a university, because it is not universal – just a name. I cannot believe it: there are Catholic universities, Mohammedan universities, Hindu universities! It seems man has gone mad. The universe is not Mohammedan, not Hindu nor Catholic. The universities should be completely free of all politics, all religions, but they should teach you the basic arts of being human – which has not been done up to now. That's why there are so many atrocities, so many inhuman acts against human beings.

What man has done to man is inconceivable. Just Adolf Hitler alone is responsible for killing at least ten million people. Joseph Stalin is not far behind. Are you going to allow all this to go on?

No, we are not going to allow it anymore.

Our ways of changing this world are certainly different. We are not going to create nuclear weapons to conquer the world and change it, no. We have already the greatest weapon in our hands: meditation.

Spread it far and wide to everyone you love, to everyone you know. Don't tell anybody that it is something to be believed in. Just say, "I experimented, and it is something not to be missed. You experiment. There is nothing to lose. If you don't get anything out of it, you have not lost anything." And it is such a simple thing that everybody, even a small child, can start doing it. It can be done even by the dying man in the last moment of his life. And if a dying man can do it, can reach his center, he will know that death is happening only to the house in which he used to live, but he is not going to die. He will know his eternity, his immortality. And that knowledge, that wisdom is the greatest richness that one can achieve.

> "We have already the greatest weapon in our hands: meditation."

No News At All

*Can you please comment on this beautiful poem by
Rumi that I love so much:
"Outside, the freezing desert night. This other night
inside grows warm, kindling. Let the landscape be
covered with thorny crust. We have a soft garden in
here. The continents blasted, cities and little towns,
everything becomes a scorched blackened ball. The
news we hear is full of grief for that future. But the
real news inside here is there's no news at all."*

The poem by Mevlana Jalaluddin Rumi is beautiful, as always. He
has spoken only beautiful words. He is one of the most significant
poets who are also mystics. That is a rare combination. There are
millions of poets in the world and there are a few mystics in the
world, but a man who is both is very rare to find.

Rumi is a very rare flower. He is as great a poet as he is a mystic.
Hence, his poetry is not just poetry, not just a beautiful arrangement
of words. It contains immense meaning and indicates toward the
ultimate truth. It is not entertainment, it is enlightenment.

He is saying:

Outside, the freezing desert night.
This other night inside grows warm, kindling.

The outside is not the real space for you to be. Outside, you are a foreigner; inside, you are at home. Outside, it is a freezing desert night. Inside, it is warm, kindling, cozy.

But very few are fortunate enough to move from the outside to the inside. They have completely forgotten that they have a home within themselves; they are searching for it but they are searching in the wrong place. They search their whole lives but always outside; they never stop for a moment and look inward.

Let the landscape be covered with thorny crust.
We have a soft garden in here.

Don't be worried about what happens on the outside. Inside, there is always a garden ready to welcome you.

The continents blasted, cities and little towns,
everything becomes a scorched, blackened ball.
The news we hear is full of grief for that future.

These words of Rumi are more significant, meaningful, today, than they were when he wrote them. He wrote them seven hundred years ago, but today it is not only a symbolic thing, it is going to become the reality:

The continents blasted, cities and little towns,
everything becomes a scorched blackened ball.
The news we hear is full of grief for that future.
But the real news inside here is there's no news at all.

This last sentence depends on an ancient saying which says: No news is good news. I was born in a very small village where the postman used to come only once a week. People were afraid that he may be bringing a letter for them; they were happy when they found that there was no letter. Once in a while, there was a telegram for someone. Just the rumor that somebody had received a telegram was such a shock in the village that everybody would gather – and only one man was educated enough to read. Everybody was afraid: a telegram? That means some bad news. Otherwise, why should you waste money on a telegram?

I learned from my very childhood that no news is good news. People were happy when they received no news from their relatives, from their friends or from anybody. That meant everything was going well.

Rumi is saying:

The news we hear is full of grief for the future.
But the real news inside, is there's no news at all.

Everything is silent and everything is as beautiful, peaceful, blissful as it has always been. There is no change at all; hence, there is no news. Inside it is an eternal ecstasy, forever and forever.

I will repeat again that these lines may become true in *your* lifetime. Before that happens, you must reach within yourself where no news has ever happened, where everything is eternally the same, where the spring never comes and goes but always remains; where flowers have been from the very beginning – if there was any beginning – and are going to remain to the very end, if there is going to be any end. In fact, there is no beginning and no end, and the garden is lush, green, and full of flowers.

Before the outside world is destroyed by your politicians, enter your inner world. That's the only safety left, the only shelter against nuclear weapons, against global suicide, against all these idiots who have so much power to destroy. But you can at least save yourself.

I was hopeful, but as the days have passed and I have become more and more acquainted with the stupidity of man… I still hope but just out of old habit; really my heart has accepted the fact that only a few people can be saved. The whole of humanity is determined to destroy itself. And these are the people that if you tell them how they can be saved, they will crucify you. They will stone you to death. Going around the world I still laugh, but there is a subtle sadness in it. I still dance with you but it is no longer with the same enthusiasm as it was ten years ago.

It seems that the higher powers of consciousness are helpless against the lower and ugly powers of politicians. The higher is always fragile, like a rose flower; you can destroy it with a stone. That does not mean that the stone becomes higher than the rose flower; it simply means the stone is unconscious of what it is doing.

The crowds are unconscious of what they are doing, and the politicians belong to the crowd. They are their representatives. When blind people are leading other blind people, it is almost impossible to wake them up; because the question is not only that they are asleep – they are blind too.

There is not time enough to cure their eyes. There is time enough to wake them but not enough time to cure their eyes. So now I have confined myself completely to my own people. That is my world, because I know those who are with me may be asleep, but they are not blind. They can be awakened.

ABOUT OSHO

Osho's unique contribution to the understanding of who we are defies categorization. Mystic and scientist, a rebellious spirit whose sole interest is to alert humanity to the urgent need to discover a new way of living. To continue as before is to invite threats to our very survival on this unique and beautiful planet.

His essential point is that only by changing ourselves, one individual at a time, can the outcome of all our "selves" – our societies, our cultures, our beliefs, our world – also change. The doorway to that change is meditation.

Osho the scientist has experimented and scrutinized all the approaches of the past and examined their effects on the modern human being and responded to their shortcomings by creating a new starting point for the hyperactive 21st Century mind: OSHO Active Meditations.

Once the agitation of a modern lifetime has started to settle, "activity" can melt into "passivity," a key starting point of real meditation. To support this next step, Osho has transformed the ancient "art of listening" into a subtle contemporary methodology: the OSHO Talks. Here words become music, the listener discovers who is listening, and the awareness moves from what is being heard to the individual doing the listening. Magically, as silence arises, what needs to be heard is understood directly, free from the distraction of a mind that can only interrupt and interfere with this delicate process.

These thousands of talks cover everything from the individual quest for meaning to the most urgent social and political issues facing society today. Osho's books are not written but are transcribed from audio and video recordings of these extemporaneous talks to international audiences. As he puts it, "So remember: whatever I am saying is not just for you...I am talking also for the future generations."

Osho has been described by *The Sunday Times* in London as one of the "1000 Makers of the 20th Century" and by American author

Tom Robbins as "the most dangerous man since Jesus Christ." *Sunday Mid-Day* (India) has selected Osho as one of ten people – along with Gandhi, Nehru and Buddha – who have changed the destiny of India.

About his own work Osho has said that he is helping to create the conditions for the birth of a new kind of human being. He often characterizes this new human being as "Zorba the Buddha" – capable both of enjoying the earthy pleasures of a Zorba the Greek and the silent serenity of a Gautama the Buddha.

Running like a thread through all aspects of Osho's talks and meditations is a vision that encompasses both the timeless wisdom of all ages past and the highest potential of today's (and tomorrow's) science and technology.

Osho is known for his revolutionary contribution to the science of inner transformation, with an approach to meditation that acknowledges the accelerated pace of contemporary life. His unique OSHO Active Meditations™ are designed to first release the accumulated stresses of body and mind, so that it is then easier to take an experience of stillness and thought-free relaxation into daily life.

Two autobiographical works by the author are available:
Autobiography of a Spiritually Incorrect Mystic,
St Martins Press, New York (book and eBook)
Glimpses of a Golden Childhood,
OSHO Media International, Pune, India (book and eBook)

OSHO INTERNATIONAL
MEDITATION RESORT

Each year the Meditation Resort welcomes thousands of people from more than 100 countries. The unique campus provides an opportunity for a direct personal experience of a new way of living – with more awareness, relaxation, celebration and creativity. A great variety of around-the-clock and around-the-year program options are available. Doing nothing and just relaxing is one of them!

All of the programs are based on Osho's vision of "Zorba the Buddha" – a qualitatively new kind of human being who is able *both* to participate creatively in everyday life *and* to relax into silence and meditation.

Location
Located 100 miles southeast of Mumbai in the thriving modern city of Pune, India, the OSHO International Meditation Resort is a holiday destination with a difference. The Meditation Resort is spread over 28 acres of spectacular gardens in a beautiful tree-lined residential area.

OSHO Meditations
A full daily schedule of meditations for every type of person includes both traditional and revolutionary methods, and particularly the OSHO Active Meditations™. The daily meditation program takes place in what must be the world's largest meditation hall, the OSHO Auditorium.

OSHO Multiversity
Individual sessions, courses and workshops cover everything from creative arts to holistic health, personal transformation, relationship

and life transition, transforming meditation into a lifestyle for life and work, esoteric sciences, and the "Zen" approach to sports and recreation. The secret of the OSHO Multiversity's success lies in the fact that all its programs are combined with meditation, supporting the understanding that as human beings we are far more than the sum of our parts.

OSHO Basho Spa
The luxurious Basho Spa provides for leisurely open-air swimming surrounded by trees and tropical green. The uniquely styled, spacious Jacuzzi, the saunas, gym, tennis courts...all these are enhanced by their stunningly beautiful setting.

Cuisine
A variety of different eating areas serve delicious Western, Asian and Indian vegetarian food – most of it organically grown especially for the Meditation Resort. Breads and cakes are baked in the resort's own bakery.

Night life
There are many evening events to choose from – dancing being at the top of the list! Other activities include full-moon meditations beneath the stars, variety shows, music performances and meditations for daily life.

Facilities
You can buy all of your basic necessities and toiletries in the Galleria. The Multimedia Gallery sells a large range of OSHO media products. There is also a bank, a travel agency and a Cyber Café on-campus. For those who enjoy shopping, Pune provides all the options, ranging from traditional and ethnic Indian products to all of the global brand-name stores.

Accommodation
You can choose to stay in the elegant rooms of the OSHO Guesthouse, or for longer stays on campus you can select

one of the OSHO Living-In programs. Additionally there is a plentiful variety of nearby hotels and serviced apartments.

www.osho.com/meditationresort
www.osho.com/guesthouse
www.osho.com/livingin

MORE BOOKS AND EBOOKS BY OSHO MEDIA INTERNATIONAL

The God Conspiracy:
The Path from Superstition to Super Consciousness

Discover the Buddha: 53 Meditations to Meet the Buddha Within
Gold Nuggets: Messages from Existence

OSHO Classics
The Book of Wisdom: The Heart of Tibetan Buddhism.
The Mustard Seed: The Revolutionary Teachings of Jesus
Ancient Music in the Pines: In Zen, Mind Suddenly Stops
The Empty Boat: Encounters with Nothingness
A Bird on the Wing: Zen Anecdotes for Everyday Life
The Path of Yoga: Discovering the Essence and Origin of Yoga
And the Flowers Showered: The Freudian Couch and Zen
Nirvana: The Last Nightmare: Learning to Trust in Life
The Goose Is Out: Zen in Action
Absolute Tao: Subtle Is the Way to Love, Happiness and Truth

The Tantra Experience: Evolution through Love
Tantric Transformation: When Love Meets Meditation

Pillars of Consciousness (illustrated)
BUDDHA: His Life and Teachings and Impact on Humanity
ZEN: Its History and Teachings and Impact on Humanity
TANTRA: The Way of Acceptance
TAO: The State and the Art

Authentic Living

Danger: Truth at Work: The Courage to Accept the Unknowable
The Magic of Self-Respect: Awakening to Your Own Awareness
Born With a Question Mark in Your Heart

OSHO eBooks and "OSHO-Singles"

Emotions: Freedom from Anger, Jealousy and Fear
Meditation: The First and Last Freedom
What Is Meditation?
The Book of Secrets: 112 Meditations to Discover the
Mystery Within

20 Difficult Things to Accomplish in This World
Compassion, Love and Sex
Hypnosis in the Service of Meditation
Why Is Communication So Difficult, Particularly between Lovers?
Bringing Up Children
Why Should I Grieve Now?: facing a loss and letting it go
Love and Hate: just two sides of the same coin

Next Time You Feel Angry...
Next Time You Feel Lonely...
Next Time You Feel Suicidal...

OSHO Media BLOG
http://oshomedia.blog.osho.com

FOR MORE INFORMATION

www.**OSHO**.com

a comprehensive multi-language website including a magazine, OSHO Books, OSHO Talks in audio and video formats, the OSHO Library text archive in English and Hindi and extensive information about OSHO Meditations. You will also find the program schedule of the OSHO Multiversity and information about the OSHO International Meditation Resort.

http://OSHO.com/AllAboutOSHO
http://OSHO.com/Resort
http://OSHO.com/Shop
http://www.youtube.com/OSHO
http://www.Twitter.com/OSHO
http://www.facebook.com/pages/OSHO.International

To contact OSHO International Foundation:
www.osho.com/oshointernational,
oshointernational@oshointernational.com